100% Middle/Junior High Mathematics Challenge

10 Practice Tests with Full Detailed Solutions

Sinan Kanbir, Ph.D.

January 2021

Copyright © 2020
MathTopia Academy
ISBN: 978-1-7356252-3-2 (paper)
ISBN: 978-1-7356252-2-5 (ebook)

Acknowledgments

I would like to thank Dursun Caliskan and Andrew Carratu for test solving and reading the drafts of this book and giving very valuable comments. I am also thankful to Suzy Lou, Stanford University Computer Science graduate student, for her willingness to proofread this book. Last, but not least, I would like to thank University of Wisconsin-Stevens Point Mathematical Sciences department faculty members, Cynthia McCabe, Daniel Harnett, Rick Mitchell, Nate Wetzel, and Mike Treuden for giving valuable feedback and always being willing to work problems in the hallways.

Possible target audiences of this book

- Participants in math contests such as AMC 8-10, MATHCOUNTS, MathCON, and Math Leagues.
- Math Circle students and organizers
- Pre-service and in-service middle school mathematics teachers.
- Parents of mathematically talented students.
- General math enthusiasts.

Contents

Preliminaries 7
Practice Exam 1 11
Practice Exam 2 21
Practice Exam 3 31
Practice Exam 4 41
Practice Exam 5 51
Practice Exam 6 61
Practice Exam 7 71
Practice Exam 8 81
Practice Exam 9 91
Practice Exam 10 101
Solutions for Practice Exam 1 113
Solutions for Practice Exam 2 123
Solutions for Practice Exam 3 131
Solutions for Practice Exam 4 138
Solutions for Practice Exam 5 146
Solutions for Practice Exam 6 155
Solutions for Practice Exam 7 165
Solutions for Practice Exam 8 172
Solutions for Practice Exam 9 181
Solutions for Practice Exam 10 190
Answers for Practice Exams 200

PRELIMINARIES

- Whole numbers = $\{0, 1, 2, \ldots, \}$
- Integers = $\{\ldots, -2, -1, 0, 1, 2, \ldots, \}$
- Positive Integers = $\{1, 2, \ldots, \}$
- Negative integers = $\{\ldots, -2, -1\}$

Divisibility. Given any two integers a and b, we say a divides b, or b is divisible by a, if there exists an integer c such that $b = a \cdot c$.

Prime Factorization. For any integer $N > 1$, there are prime numbers $p_1, p_2, \ldots, p_k$ and positive integers $a_1, a_2, \ldots, a_k$ such that $N = p_1^{a_1} p_2^{a_2} \cdots p_k^{a_k}$.

Number of positive divisors. Given a number $N = p_1^{a_1} p_2^{a_2} \cdots p_k^{a_k}$ in prime factorization form, the number of positive divisors of N is $(a_1 + 1)(a_2 + 1) \ldots (a_k + 1)$.

Telescopic Sums. For a positive integer n:
$$\sum_{i=1}^{n} 1 = n \qquad \sum_{i=1}^{n} k = \frac{n(n+1)}{2}$$
$$\sum_{i=1}^{2n+1} (2k+1) = n^2$$
$$\sum_{i=1}^{n} k(k+1) = \frac{n(n+1)(n+2)}{3}$$
$$\sum_{i=1}^{n} k(k+1)(k+2) = \frac{n(n+1)(n+2)(n+3)}{4}$$

Factorial. For any positive integer n, it is defined as $n! = 1 \cdot 2 \cdots n$. It is assumed that $0! = 1$.

Permutation. n different objects can be arranged into k in $P(n, k) = \dfrac{n!}{(n-k)!}$ ways.

Circular Permutation. n different people can be sit on a rounded table in $(n-1)!$ ways.

Combination. The number of ways to choose k objects from n different objects is
$$C(n, k) = \binom{n}{k} = \frac{n!}{k! \cdot (n-k)!}.$$

Number of solutions. For some positive integers n and k, consider the equation
$$a_1 + a_2 + \ldots + a_k = n$$
Then, it has $C(n - k - 1, k - 1)$ solutions in non-negative integers. As a result, it has $C(n - 1, k - 1)$ solutions in positive integers.

Conditional Probability. The probability of X given that Y is
$$\Pr(X|Y) = \frac{\Pr(X \cap Y)}{\Pr(Y)}.$$

Some Geometry Notations.
A	Point A
$\overleftrightarrow{AB}$	Line through points A and B
$\overline{AB}$	Line segment joining A and B
AB	Length of the line segment $\overline{AB}$.
$\angle ABC$	Angle with the vertex point at B
$m\angle ABC$	Measure of $\angle ABC$
$\perp$	Perpendicular
$\parallel$	Parallel

Angle Bisector Theorem.

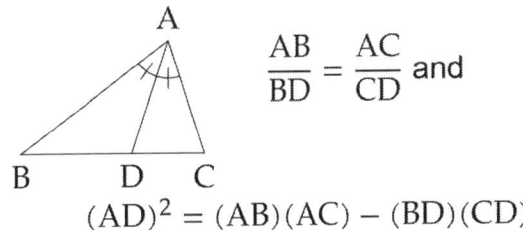

$$\frac{AB}{BD} = \frac{AC}{CD} \text{ and}$$
$$(AD)^2 = (AB)(AC) - (BD)(CD)$$

Heron's formula. The area of a triangle with side lengths a, b and c is
$$\sqrt{u(u-a)(u-b)(u-c)}$$
where $u = (a + b + c)/2$.

Practice Exams

Practice Exam 1

- You have **75 minutes** for **25 problems**.

- There are no penalties for incorrect answers. Answer as many problems as you can; return to the others in the time you have left for the test.

Problem 1. In the diagram, each of the five boxes is to contain a number. Each of the three numbers in the three middle boxes (including 28) is equal to the average of the number to its left and the number to its right. What number must occupy the box labeled e?

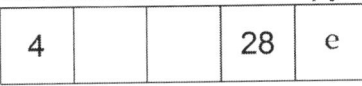

A) 32   B) 34   C) 36   D) 38   E) None of the preceding

Problem 2. If a is an even positive integer and b is an odd positive integer, which of the following could represent an odd integer?

A) $a \cdot b$ B) $a + 2b$ C) $a^b + 1$ D) $a + b + 1$ E) $a - b + 1$

Practice Exam 1

Problem 3. A cube of edge length 4 cm is painted green on all faces. It is then cut into 64 identical unit cubes. How many unit cubes have paint on exactly two faces?

A) 24   B) 28   C) 32   D) 36   E) None of the preceding

Problem 4. How many different isosceles triangles have integer side lengths and perimeter 17?

A) 3   B) 4   C) 5   D) 6   E) 8

Problem 5. In the addition problem below, the letters A and B represent different digits. What is the value of $A + B$?

A) 12
B) 13
C) 14
D) 15
E) 16

```
      7  7  B
      5  A  B
  +   A  A  B
  ─────────────
   1  8  B  7
```

Practice Exam 1

Problem 6. An integer N has 10 positive divisors. If $2N$ has 15 positive divisors and $3N$ has 20 positive divisors, how many positive divisors does $4N$ have?

A) 12   B) 20   C) 30   D) 36   E) 40

Problem 7. The points in the 3×3 grid below are equally spaced horizontally and vertically. How many squares of any size can be formed by connecting four of the points?

A) 14
B) 15
C) 18
D) 20
E) 21

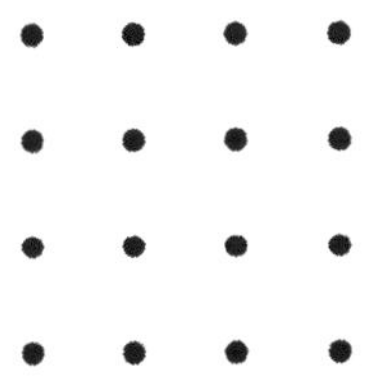

Problem 8. In a convex pentagon $ABCDE$, $m\angle A = 40°$, $m\angle B = m\angle E$ and $m\angle C = m\angle D$. What is the sum of the measures of $\angle B$ and $\angle C$?

A) 225°   B) 230°   C) 240°   D) 250°   E) Cannot be determined

Practice Exam 1

Problem 9. A *magic* number represents the number of dots in a rectangle containing two more rows than columns. The first four magic numbers are 3, 8, 15, and 24. What is the 20th magic number?

A) 341
B) 360
C) 399
D) 440
E) 489

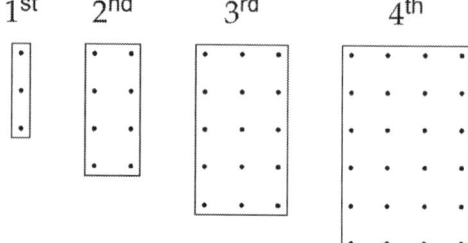

Problem 10. What is the units digit of $2^{2020} \cdot 7^{2020}$?

A) 2 B) 4 C) 6 D) 8 E) 9

Problem 11. Two brothers and two sisters stand side-by-side for a photograph. The two sisters refuse to stand next to each other. How many different ways can they be arranged for the photo?

A) 12 B) 15 C) 16 D) 18 E) 24

Problem 12. Point O is the center of the semicircle where $OD = DB$, $AB \perp CD$, $CD = 2\sqrt{3}$ and $m\angle CAB = 30°$. What is the radius of the circle?

A) 4
B) $3\sqrt{2}$
C) 5
D) $3\sqrt{3}$
E) 6

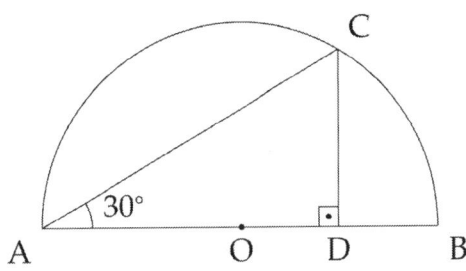

Problem 13. An 8×10 rectangle is made of 1×1 squares. How many 1×1 squares are needed to represent 0.725 times the area of the whole rectangle?

A) 56
B) 58
C) 60
D) 62
E) 64

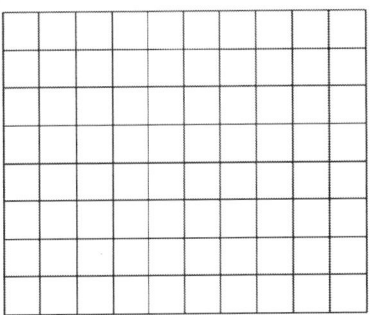

Problem 14. Robert writes down a list of whole numbers beginning with 1. To generate the next number in the list, he either adds 6 to the previous number, or he multiplies the previous number by 4. For example, his list could be the sequence 1, 7, 28, 34, 40, 160, ...Which of the following numbers *cannot* appear in Robert's sequence?

A) 109   B) 151   C) 244   D) 335   E) 412

Practice Exam 1

Problem 15. In a regular octagon, all diagonals are drawn. If a diagonal is chosen at random, what is the probability that it is either one of the shortest or one of the longest?

A) $\frac{2}{5}$ B) $\frac{3}{5}$ C) $\frac{12}{25}$ D) $\frac{4}{5}$ E) None of the preceding

Problem 16. Two identical regular hexagons are drawn in a rectangle as given in the figure. If the area of each hexagon is 6 in², what is the area of the rectangle?

A) 18 in²

B) 21 in²

C) 24 in²

D) 27 in²

E) None of the preceding

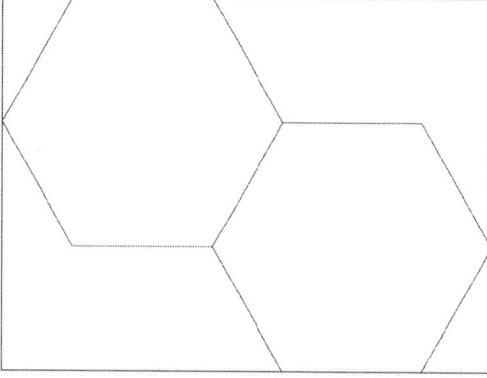

Problem 17. Alfred, Benjamin, and Carl have a total of 252 trading cards. Alfred gives one-fifth of his cards to Benjamin. Benjamin then gives some of his cards to Carl. After this process, all three people have the same number of cards, and Carl has twice as many cards as he had originally. How many cards did Benjamin have originally?

A) 42   B) 70   C) 84   D) 105   E) 147

Practice Exam 1

Problem 18. What is the sum of all integers x which make the expression $\dfrac{2002}{2x-7}$ an integer?

A) −51 B) −32 C) 56 D) 51 E) 0

Problem 19. A doughnut shop offers four flavors of doughnuts: glazed, chocolate, strawberry, and cinnamon. Albert wishes to buy 12 doughnuts, including at least one doughnut of each flavor. How many possible combinations of donuts can Albert buy? (For example, Albert may buy 2 glazed, 5 chocolate, 3 strawberry, and 2 cinnamon doughnuts.)

A) 165 B) 220 C) 286 D) 330 E) 455

Problem 20. The area of the triangle formed by the x-axis, y-axis, and the line $2y = mx + 6$ is 36. What is $|m|$?

A) $\dfrac{1}{16}$ B) $\dfrac{1}{8}$ C) $\dfrac{1}{4}$ D) $\dfrac{3}{4}$ E) $\dfrac{4}{3}$

Practice Exam 1

Problem 21. If x and y are real numbers so that $4x^2 + y^4 - 4y^2 - 20x + 29 = 0$, then what is the value of $y^2 + 2x$?

    A) 5   B) 7   C) 9   D) 15   E) 29

Problem 22. Suppose xx, yy and zz are two-digit whole numbers. If $x^2 + y^2 + z^2 = 74$ then find the number of positive divisors of $(xx)^2 + (yy)^2 + (zz)^2$.

    A) 6   B) 8   C) 10   D) 12   E) None of the preceding

Problem 23. In how many ways can a blank 3×3 grid be filled with the integers from 1 to 9 so that squares containing consecutive integers are adjacent (i.e., have a common edge)? <u>Hint:</u> Of the three examples below, **A** and **B** satisfy the given conditions, while **C** does not because the squares containing 1 and 2 are not adjacent!

A) 28
B) 32
C) 36
D) 40
E) None of the preceding

9	8	7
2	1	6
3	4	5

A

7	8	9
6	5	4
1	2	3

B

1	3	2
6	5	4
7	8	9

C

Problem 24. In trapezoid ABCD, $\overline{AB} \parallel \overline{DC}$ and $m\angle DAB = 2m\angle ABC$. Given that $AD = DC = 1$ and $AB = 3$, what is BC?

A) 2 B) $\dfrac{5}{2}$ C) $\sqrt{3}$ D) $\sqrt{6}$ E) $\dfrac{7}{2}$

Problem 25. Suppose a and b are real numbers such that $ab^2 = 1$ and $a^3 + 3b^3 = 4$. What is the product of all possible values of $a^3 + b^3$?

A) 12 B) 18 C) 24 D) 36 E) 72

Assessment for Practice Exam 1

Q #	Topic	YA	CA	☑ ☒ ☐	Notes
1	Algebra				
2	Number Theory				
3	Combinatorics				
4	Geometry				
5	Algebra				
6	Number Theory				
7	Combinatorics				
8	Geometry				
9	Algebra				
10	Number Theory				
11	Combinatorics				
12	Geometry				
13	Algebra				
14	Number Theory				
15	Combinatorics				
16	Geometry				
17	Algebra				
18	Number Theory				
19	Combinatorics				
20	Geometry				
21	Algebra				
22	Number Theory				
23	Combinatorics				
24	Geometry				
25	Algebra				

CA: Correct Answer   YA: Your Answer   ☑ Correct   ☒ Incorrect   ☐ Empty

Practice Exam 2

- You have **75 minutes** for **25 problems**.

- There are no penalties for incorrect answers. Answer as many problems as you can; return to the others in the time you have left for the test.

Problem 1. If $x + 4 = y^2 - 1 = z^2 + 2 = t - 3 = m^2 + 12$, which of the numbers x, y, z, t, and m is the greatest?

A) x B) y C) z D) t E) m

Problem 2. Suppose a and b are integers and $a + b$ is an odd number. Which of the following is always true?

    I) $a - 2b$ is even   II) $a \cdot b$ is even   III) $4a + b$ is even

A) Only I B) Only II C) Only III D) I and II E) I, II and III

Practice Exam 2

Problem 3. How many ways can the letters of the word TRIANGLE be arranged such that the letters ANGLE appear consecutively, and in that order?

    A) 6   B) 18   C) 20   D) 24   E) 56

Problem 4. What is the area of an isosceles triangle with side lengths 10, 10, and 12?

    A) 48   B) 50   C) 60   D) 72   E) 96

Problem 5. In an online math practice test, Junaid attempts exactly $\frac{3}{4}$ of the problems and answers $\frac{5}{8}$ of those problems correctly. When he submits the test, he finds that he answered 105 problems correctly. How many math problems were on this test?

    A) 220   B) 224   C) 243   D) 248   E) None of the preceding

Problem 6. Distinct, nonzero digits A, B, and C are such that the three-digit numbers ABC, CAB, and BCA are divisible by 4, 5, and 9, respectively. What is the greatest possible value of A × B × C?

A) 20   B) 180   C) 200   D) 210   E) 240

Problem 7. Set A = {−7, −6, −5, −4, −3, −2, −1, 1, 2, 3}. What is the probability that product of two randomly selected numbers is positive number?

A) $\frac{1}{15}$ B) $\frac{4}{15}$ C) $\frac{7}{15}$ D) $\frac{8}{15}$ E) $\frac{14}{15}$

Problem 8. A rectangular box has integer side lengths in the ratio of $1 : \frac{3}{2} : 2$. Which of the following could be the volume of the box?

A) 136   B) 148   C) 160   D) 192   E) 204

Practice Exam 2

Problem 9. If $A = \dfrac{21}{19} + \dfrac{11}{29}$, then which of the following equals $\dfrac{18}{29} - \dfrac{2}{19}$?

A) $2 - A$ B) $1 - A$ C) A D) $A + 1$ E) $A + 2$

Problem 10. The first page number of a book is 1. The sum of page numbers in the book is less than 2020. If there were 1 more page, then the sum of page numbers in the book would be more than 2020. Find the number of pages of the book.

A) 59   B) 60   C) 61   D) 62   E) 63

Problem 11. Alice and Bob each roll a fair 12-sided die. What is the probability that Alice's roll is greater than or equal to Bob's roll?

A) $\dfrac{11}{24}$ B) $\dfrac{1}{2}$ C) $\dfrac{25}{48}$ D) $\dfrac{13}{24}$ E) $\dfrac{7}{12}$

Problem 12. The diagram shows four identical rectangles placed inside a square. The perimeter of each rectangle is 24 cm. What is the perimeter of the large square?

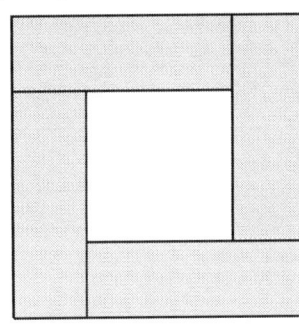

A) 24 cm

B) 30 cm

C) 36 cm

D) 48 cm

E) 56 cm

Problem 13. The fraction $\frac{7}{13}$ is equal to $0.\overline{538461} = 0.5384615384615....$ What is the 2020th digit to the right of the decimal point?

A) 1   B) 3   C) 4   D) 5   E) 6

Problem 14. If $N = 2^3 \cdot 3^2 \cdot 7 \cdot n$, and N is divisible by 50, then which of the following *could* be the value of n?

A) 5   B) 15   C) 20   D) 40   E) 75

Practice Exam 2

Problem 15. In a school of 300 students, there are 38 people on the football team and 30 people on the basketball team. If there are 252 students who play neither sport, how many students are on both teams?

    A) 20   B) 24   C) 28   D) 32   E) None

Problem 16. The ratio of the corresponding side lengths of two similar triangles is $5:4$, and the perimeter of the larger triangle is 30 cm. What is length the of the shortest side of the smaller triangle, if its side lengths are consecutive even numbers?

    A) 10 cm   B) 8 cm   C) 6 cm   D) 4 cm   E) 2 cm

Problem 17. In the grid below, each of the 16 squares is to be filled with either 0 or 1 so that the sum of the four numbers in each row and column is even. In how many ways can this be done?

A) 2^9
B) 2^{10}
C) 2^{12}
D) 2^{15}
E) 2^{16}

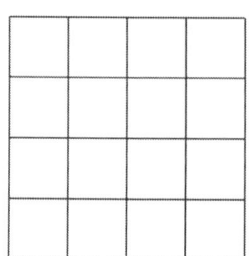

Practice Exam 2

Problem 18. What is the number of ordered pairs (x, y) of positive integers that satisfy the equation?
$$2x + 3y = 120$$

A) 19 B) 24 C) 29 D) 36 E) None

Problem 19. If $x, y,$ and z are three numbers picked randomly and with replacement from the set $\{1, 2, 3, 4, 5\}$ then what is the probability that $xz + y$ is even number?

A) $\dfrac{2}{5}$ B) $\dfrac{23}{25}$ C) $\dfrac{39}{125}$ D) $\dfrac{64}{125}$ E) $\dfrac{59}{125}$

Problem 20. Point P is on the same plane as $\triangle ABC$. For how many P are $\triangle PAB$, $\triangle PAC$, and $\triangle PBC$ isosceles?

A) 1 B) 6 C) 7 D) 10 E) 12

Practice Exam 2

Problem 21. The real numbers a and b satisfy $a + b = 2$ and $a \cdot b = -1$. What is the value of

$$\frac{1}{a} + \frac{a^2}{b^3} + \frac{1}{b} + \frac{b^2}{a^3}?$$

A) −76 B) −80 C) −84 D) −88 E) None of the preceding

Problem 22. What is the number of integer solutions (x, y) satisfying the equation

$$x \cdot y = 3x + 6y?$$

A) 0 B) 9 C) 12 D) 16 E) 18

Problem 23. Gabby lives in a town whose streets are on a grid system with all streets running east-west or north-south without breaks. Her school, located on a corner, lies four blocks south and three blocks east of her home, also located on a corner. If Gabby only walks south or east on her way to school, how many possible routes can she take to school?

A) 20
B) 25
C) 30
D) 35
E) 40

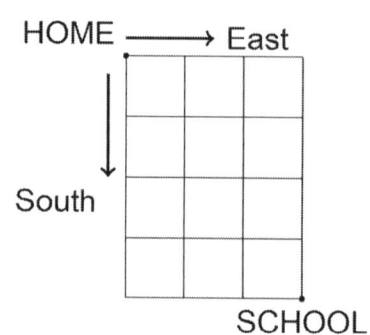

Practice Exam 2

Problem 24. ABC is a right triangle with AB ⊥ AC and AD is angle bisector of ∠BAC. If AD = 1, what is the value of $\frac{1}{AB} + \frac{1}{AC}$?

A) $\sqrt{2}$　　　B) $\frac{3}{2}$　　　C) $\sqrt{2}+1$　　　D) $\frac{1+\sqrt{5}}{2}$　　　E) None of the preceding

Problem 25. Three of 101 coins are fake. Weights of the fake coins are equivalent and lighter than the real coins. What is the minimum number of weightings to guarantee that we can find 25 real coins by using an equal arm balance?

A) 2　　　B) 3　　　C) 4　　　D) 5　　　E) None

Assessment for Practice Exam 2

Q #	Topic	YA	CA	☑ ☒ ☐	Notes
1	Algebra				
2	Number Theory				
3	Combinatorics				
4	Geometry				
5	Algebra				
6	Number Theory				
7	Combinatorics				
8	Geometry				
9	Algebra				
10	Number Theory				
11	Combinatorics				
12	Geometry				
13	Algebra				
14	Number Theory				
15	Combinatorics				
16	Geometry				
17	Algebra				
18	Number Theory				
19	Combinatorics				
20	Geometry				
21	Algebra				
22	Number Theory				
23	Combinatorics				
24	Geometry				
25	Algebra				

CA: Correct Answer   YA: Your Answer   ☑ Correct   ☒ Incorrect   ☐ Empty

Practice Exam 3

- You have **75 minutes** for **25 problems**.

- There are no penalties for incorrect answers. Answer as many problems as you can; return to the others in the time you have left for the test.

Problem 1. The sum of all integers from -13 to 14 (including -13 and 14) is A. The product of all these integers is B. Find $A + B$.

A) 0 B) 13 C) 14 D) 12584 E) None of the preceding

Problem 2. For how many positive values of n are both $\frac{n}{3}$ and $3n$ three digit integers?

A) 12 B) 15 C) 18 D) 21 E) 24

Practice Exam 3

Problem 3. The number 800 can be written as the product of two positive even integers. In how many ways can this be done?

 A) 8 B) 7 C) 6 D) 5 E) 4

Problem 4. What is the degree measure of the smaller angle formed by the hands of a clock at 8:15?

 A) 150° B) 157.5° C) 165° D) 172.5° E) None of the preceding

Problem 5. There are 19 figures consisting of triangles and squares. They have 68 edges in total. How many triangles are there?

 A) 8 B) 9 C) 10 D) 11 E) 12

Practice Exam 3

Problem 6. The five-digit number 3M8M5 is divisible by 9. What is the value of the digit M?

A) 0   B) 1   C) 2   D) 3   E) 4

Problem 7. Three fair six-sided dice are rolled. What is the probability that the three dice all show the same number?

A) $\dfrac{1}{216}$ B) $\dfrac{1}{36}$ C) $\dfrac{1}{18}$ D) $\dfrac{1}{6}$ E) None of the preceding

Problem 8. A cube is inscribed in a sphere. If the volume of the cube is 8, what is the surface area of the sphere?

A) $15\pi\sqrt{3}$ B) $12\pi\sqrt{2}$ C) 15π D) 12π E) None of the preceding

Practice Exam 3

Problem 9. A restaurant offers four desserts, and exactly twice as many appetizers as main courses. A dinner consists of an appetizer, a main course, and a dessert. What is the least number of main courses that the restaurant should offer so that a customer could have a different dinner each night for a year?

    A) 5   B) 6   C) 7   D) 8   E) 9

Problem 10. The number 100 has nine factors: 1, 2, 4, 5, 10, 20, 25, 50, and 100. How many factors does 900 have?

    A) 11   B) 18   C) 27   D) 45   E) 81

Problem 11. Five companies each send three representatives to a networking event. At the event, each representative must shake hands with all the representatives from companies other than their own. How many handshakes must take place?

    A) 72   B) 90   C) 108   D) 120   E) 156

Problem 12. Suppose $\overline{BD}$ bisects $\angle ABC$, $\overline{AC} \cap \overline{BD} = \{E\}$, $m\angle ACB = 50°$, and $m\angle ACD = 65°$. What is the value of $m\angle ADB$?

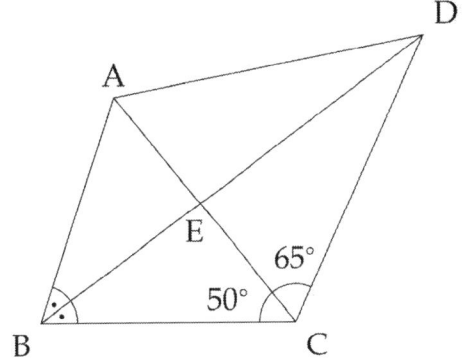

A) 20°

B) 25°

C) 30°

D) 35°

E) None of the preceding

Problem 13. How many minutes between 3:59 p.m. and 4:59 p.m. on the same day will all three digits in a digital clock display be even?

A) 10   B) 12   C) 14   D) 15   E) 16

Problem 14. How many digits are there in the number $125^4 \cdot 64^2$, when expressed as a base-10 integer?

A) 10   B) 11   C) 12   D) 13   E) 14

Practice Exam 3

Problem 15. A *palindrome* is a positive whole number which reads the same forwards and backwards. For example, 7, 11, and 252 are all palindromes. How many *palindromes* are less than 1,000?

    A) 81   B) 90   C) 99   D) 108   E) 126

Problem 16. Equilateral $\triangle ADE$ shares a side with square ADCF. What is the sum of $m\angle FEC$ and $m\angle DEC$?

A) 195°
B) 200°
C) 215°
D) 225°
E) 245°

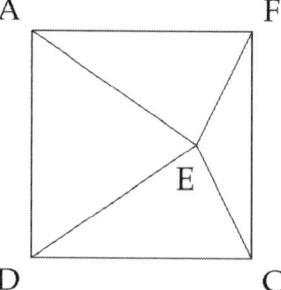

Problem 17. If a and b are positive integers with $(b-1)^{a+b} = 2^6$, then the number of possible values for a is

    A) 1   B) 2   C) 3   D) 4   E) 6

Problem 18. $T(n)$ is the sum of the digits of the positive integer n. (e.g. $T(5081) = 5 + 0 + 8 + 1 = 14$) Find the number n that satisfies $T(n) + 3n = 2020$.

A) 666 B) 667 C) 668 D) 669 E) None of the preceding

Problem 19. In a regular decagon, all diagonals are drawn. If a diagonal is chosen at random, what is the probability it is neither one of the shortest nor one of the longest?

A) $\frac{2}{7}$ B) $\frac{3}{7}$ C) $\frac{12}{35}$ D) $\frac{4}{9}$ E) $\frac{4}{7}$

Problem 20. ABCD is a convex pentagon with $m\angle B = m\angle D = 90°$ and $m\angle C = 120°$. Given that $AB = 4$, $BC = CD = 2\sqrt{3}$, and $ED = 2$, what is AE?

A) $\sqrt{3}$ B) $\frac{3}{2}$ C) $\frac{3\sqrt{3}}{2}$ D) $2\sqrt{3}$ E) None of the preceding

Practice Exam 3

Problem 21. x is a real number satisfying $(x-3)^{x^2-9} = 1$. What is the sum of all possible values of x?

A) 1   B) 3   C) 4   D) 7   E) 8

Problem 22. If a, b and c are distinct prime numbers with $a - c = 5094$ and $a + b + c = 5242$, then what is the value of $a + 2b$?

A) 5167   B) 5171   C) 5176   D) 6002   E) None of the preceding

Problem 23. 5 soccer teams participate in a tournament. Each team plays all the other teams exactly once. If a team wins a game, 3 points are awarded. If a team loses a game, no points are awarded. If the game is tie, both teams get 1 point. At the end of all the games, 4 of the 5 teams get 1, 2, 5, and 8 points in total. What is the total score of the fifth team?

A) 10   B) 12   C) 14   D) 16   E) None

Problem 24. ABC is a triangle with integer side lengths and AC = 56. Point D is on BC such that AD is angle bisector of ∠BAC. Given that AB = DC, what is BC?

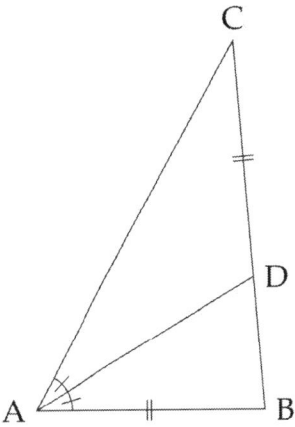

A) 42
B) 48
C) 66
D) 70
E) 72

Problem 25. How many pairs (x, y) of positive integers are there so that $3x + 5y = 613$?

A) 23   B) 29   C) 35   D) 41   E) 45

Assessment for Practice Exam 3

Q #	Topic	YA	CA	☑ ☒ ☐	Notes
1	Algebra				
2	Number Theory				
3	Combinatorics				
4	Geometry				
5	Algebra				
6	Number Theory				
7	Combinatorics				
8	Geometry				
9	Algebra				
10	Number Theory				
11	Combinatorics				
12	Geometry				
13	Algebra				
14	Number Theory				
15	Combinatorics				
16	Geometry				
17	Algebra				
18	Number Theory				
19	Combinatorics				
20	Geometry				
21	Algebra				
22	Number Theory				
23	Combinatorics				
24	Geometry				
25	Algebra				

CA: Correct Answer YA: Your Answer ☑ Correct ☒ Incorrect ☐ Empty

Practice Exam 4

- You have **75 minutes** for **25 problems**.

- There are no penalties for incorrect answers. Answer as many problems as you can; return to the others in the time you have left for the test.

Problem 1. Which of the following is equal to $\dfrac{3^8 + 3^8 + 3^8}{9^4 + 9^4 + 9^4}$?

A) $\dfrac{1}{2}$ B) $\dfrac{1}{3}$ C) 1   D) 3   E) None of the preceding

Problem 2. The sequence 1, 8, 27, 64, ..., ends with 1,000,000. How many terms are in the sequence?

A) 99   B) 100   C) 999   D) 1000   E) 10001

Practice Exam 4

Problem 3. In a class, 10 students use social media A, 9 students use social media B, 6 students use both social media A and social media B, and 2 students use neither social media A nor social media B. What is the probability of selecting a student from this class at random who uses only social media B?

A) $\dfrac{1}{5}$ B) $\dfrac{4}{15}$ C) $\dfrac{2}{5}$ D) $\dfrac{3}{5}$ E) $\dfrac{1}{15}$

Problem 4. At 6:30, what is the acute angle formed by the minute hand and hour hand of a 12-hour clock?

A) 10° B) 15° C) 20° D) 25° E) 30°

Problem 5. x, y and z are three numbers such that $x - y = y + z = 3$ and $y \neq 0$. What is the value of $\dfrac{x^2 - z^2}{y}$?

A) 4 B) 6 C) 10 D) 12 E) The answer depends on y.

Practice Exam 4

Problem 6. For how many whole numbers x is $\dfrac{12}{x+2}$ an integer?

A) 12 B) 10 C) 8 D) 6 E) 5

Problem 7. Students at Taylor Swift Middle School are assigned identification numbers with a capital letter followed by three digits, such as E482 or Q635. How many different identification numbers are possible?

A) 10,000 B) 20,000 C) 24,000 D) 26,000 E) 36,000

Problem 8. The vertices of a triangle are (1,1), (5,4), and (3,4). What is the area of the triangle?

A) 3 B) $\dfrac{7}{2}$ C) 4 D) $\dfrac{9}{2}$ E) 5

Practice Exam 4

Problem 9. Suppose x and y are integers with $3^{2x} - 4^y = 77$. What is the value of $x + y$?

A) 2 B) 3 C) 4 D) 5 E) 7

Problem 10. For how many integers n is $|n^2 - 6n + 5|$ prime?

A) 1 B) 2 C) 3 D) 4 E) 5

Problem 11. Start with 243. In each blank below, insert either ×3 or ÷9 to create a true equation. How many different true equations can be formed?

$$243 \; \underline{\quad} \; \underline{\quad} \; \underline{\quad} \; \underline{\quad} \; \underline{\quad} \; \underline{\quad} \; \underline{\quad} \; = 1$$

A) 5 B) 12 C) 35 D) 128 E) 256

Practice Exam 4

Problem 12. Given that ABCDEFGH is a regular octagon, what is m∠AGH?

A) 15°   B) 22.5°   C) 25°   D) 27.5°   E) 30°

Problem 13. The first page number of a book is 1. The sum of page numbers of the book is less than 4040. If there were 1 more page, then the sum of page numbers of the book would be more than 4040. Find the number of pages of the book.

A) 89   B) 90   C) 91   D) 90   E) 93

Problem 14. Suppose x and y are integers such that $x(y+1) = 8$ and $y(x+1) = 9$. What is the smallest value of $x + y$?

A) −7   B) −4   C) −3   D) 4   E) None of the preceding

Practice Exam 4

Problem 15. A point X is selected uniformly at random inside square ABCD with side length 6. What is the probability that the area that the area of the quadrilateral ABXD is greater than 18?

A) $\frac{1}{6}$ B) $\frac{1}{4}$ C) $\frac{1}{3}$ D) $\frac{1}{2}$ E) $\frac{6}{19}$

Problem 16. Let ABC be acute triangle. If the angles of ABC, in degrees, are integers and form an arithmetic sequence . How many different possible triangles can be formed?

A) 30   B) 31   C) 33   D) 34   E) 36

Problem 17. What is the sum of all real values x which satisfy the following equation?

$$\left(\frac{x}{2} - 3\right)^{x+2} = 1$$

A) 6   B) 7   C) 8   D) 10   E) 12

Problem 18. How many ordered integer pairs (x, y) satisfy the following equation?

$$(y + x)(y - x) = 111 + 6y$$

A) 2 B) 4 C) 8 D) 12 E) 16

Problem 19. Two different whole numbers are randomly selected from the set $\{1, 2, 3, \ldots, 10\}$. What is the probability that their product is an even number?

A) $\frac{2}{9}$ B) $\frac{5}{9}$ C) $\frac{2}{3}$ D) $\frac{3}{4}$ E) $\frac{7}{9}$

Problem 20. ABCD is a parallelogram. $CE = 3 \cdot ED$, $BF = FC$ and $KF = 6$. Find AK.

A) 10
B) 12
C) 14
D) 15
E) 16

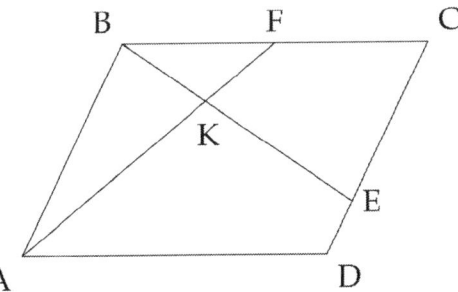

Practice Exam 4

Problem 21. If $a^2 = 2020$, then what is the exact value of $\dfrac{a^3 - 3a^2 - a + 3}{a - 3}$?

A) 2018 B) 2019 C) 2020^2 D) $2020^3 - 2020^2$ E) None of the preceding

Problem 22. What is the sum of all positive integers $n \neq 3$ such that the quantity $\dfrac{n^3 - 3}{n - 3}$ is an integer?

A) 27 B) 34 C) 60 D) 84 E) 87

Problem 23. How many ordered triples (a, b, c) of positive integers are solutions to the inequality $a + b + c \leq 20$?

A) 171 B) 231 C) 1140 D) 1771 E) None of the preceding

Problem 24. For a triangle ABC, suppose the bisector of ∠ABC intersects AC at the point D. If $BD = 3\sqrt{5}$, $AB = 8$, and $CD = \frac{3}{2}$, what is $AD + BC$?

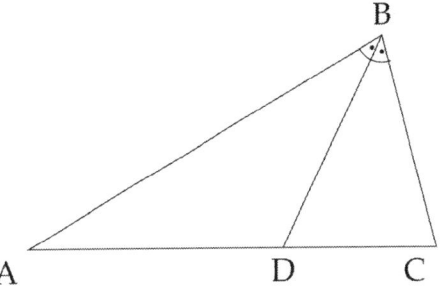

A) 4

B) 6

C) 8

D) 10

E) None of the preceding

Problem 25. Suppose p_1, p_2, and p_3 are prime numbers that satisfy $p_1 + p_2 = (p_1 - p_2 + p_3) \cdot p_3$ and $p_1 + p_2 \leq 60$. What is the maximum value of $p_1 \cdot p_2 \cdot p_3$?

A) Between 201 and 300

B) Between 601 and 700

C) Between 701 and 800

D) Between 801 and 900

E) None of the preceding

Assessment for Practice Exam 4

Q #	Topic	YA	CA	☑ ☒ ☐	Notes
1	Algebra				
2	Number Theory				
3	Combinatorics				
4	Geometry				
5	Algebra				
6	Number Theory				
7	Combinatorics				
8	Geometry				
9	Algebra				
10	Number Theory				
11	Combinatorics				
12	Geometry				
13	Algebra				
14	Number Theory				
15	Combinatorics				
16	Geometry				
17	Algebra				
18	Number Theory				
19	Combinatorics				
20	Geometry				
21	Algebra				
22	Number Theory				
23	Combinatorics				
24	Geometry				
25	Algebra				

CA: Correct Answer   YA: Your Answer   ☑ Correct   ☒ Incorrect   ☐ Empty

Practice Exam 5

♦ You have **75 minutes** for **25 problems**.

♦ There are no penalties for incorrect answers. Answer as many problems as you can; return to the others in the time you have left for the test.

Problem 1. Ashley and Kim want to begin a jogging routine. The local park's trail is only 30% of Ashley's distance goal and 50% of Kim's, so instead of jogging together, they decide to each jog from their homes to the library, play a game of chess, and each jog back home, which will exactly meet each runner's goal. If Ashley lives 1.8 miles from the library, how far from the library does Kim live?

A) 0.54 miles   B) 0.6 miles   C) 1.08 miles   D) 1.1 miles   E) 1.2 miles

Problem 2. Suppose x and y are positive integers such that $26 \cdot 27 \cdot 28 \cdot ... \cdot 100 = 5^x \cdot y$. What is the largest possible value of x?

A) 15   B) 16   C) 17   D) 18   E) 19

Practice Exam 5

Problem 3. All two digit numbers are written on different cards and put in a drawing box. When you draw one card, what is the probability that at most two of the digits are 3?

A) $\frac{1}{9}$ B) $\frac{1}{5}$ C) $\frac{1}{30}$ D) $\frac{1}{15}$ E) 1

Problem 4. Given a triangle ABC, the angle bisector of ∠BAC intersects $\overline{BC}$ at the point D. If m∠ADB = 80° and m∠B = 2m∠C, what is the value of m∠B?

A) 20°
B) 25°
C) 30°
D) 35°
E) 40°

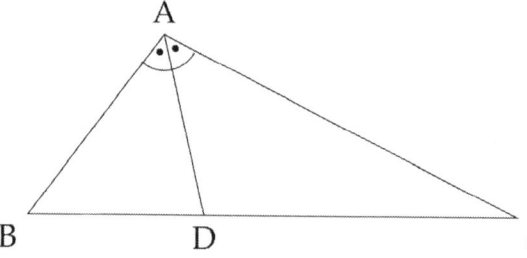

Problem 5. Suppose a and b are non-zero additive inverses (opposites) of each other. What is the value of the following expression?

$$2(a+b-1)^{2019} + 3\left(\frac{a}{b}\right)^{2020} + 2019$$

A) 1 B) 2017 C) 2019 D) 2020 E) None of the preceding

Problem 6. The pages of the book Mathtopia are numbered from 1. The page numbers have a total of 459 digits. How many pages does the book have?

A) 119   B) 189   C) 190   D) 215   E) 219

Problem 7. How many three-digit numbers with all digits greater than zero and digit sum 11 are there?

A) 27   B) 33   C) 39   D) 45   E) None of the preceding

Problem 8. The diagram shows four identical rectangles placed inside a square. The perimeter of each identical rectangle is 24, and the perimeter of the center square is 20. What is the sum of the areas of the outer rectangles (border area)?

A) 110

B) 120

C) 124

D) 136

E) None of the preceding

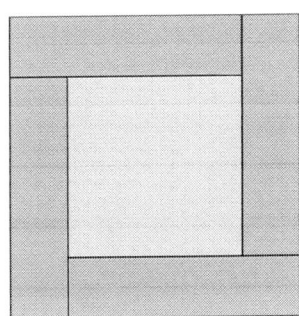

Practice Exam 5

Problem 9. If $2^{2018} - 2^{2017} - 2^{2016} + 2^{2015} = a \cdot 2^{2015}$, what is the value of a?

A) 3   B) 5   C) 8   D) 13   E) 16

Problem 10. Let a and b be digits such that the eight-digit number aaaabbbb is a multiple of 45. What is the sum of all possible values of a?

A) 11   B) 13   C) 14   D) 15   E) 17

Problem 11. A box has 6 red, 4 blue, and 7 green balls. How many balls must be drawn from the box to make sure that 1 red ball is selected?

A) 10   B) 11   C) 12   D) 13   E) 14

Problem 12. Suppose ABCDEF is a regular hexagon with side length $2\sqrt{3}$. Find the area of $\triangle AEC$.

A) $9\sqrt{3}$
B) 12
C) $12\sqrt{2}$
D) $12\sqrt{3}$
E) None of the preceding

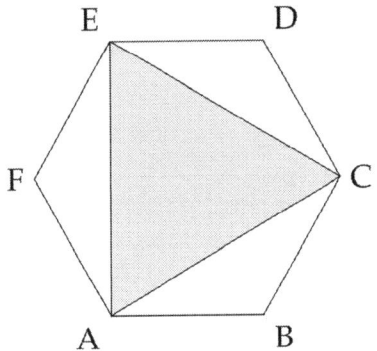

Problem 13. How many integers n satisfy the compound inequality $\frac{1}{4} \le \frac{n}{2019} \le \frac{1}{3}$?

A) 150 B) 160 C) 167 D) 169 E) None of the preceding

Problem 14. Let a and b are positive numbers such that $A = a^2 - b^2$ and A is a prime number. Which of the following would be the value of $a + b$?

A) 15 B) 23 C) 33 D) 45 E) 91

Practice Exam 5

Problem 15. How many even positive integers have their digits in strictly increasing order, when read left-to-right? Two examples include 8 and 12456, but not 334.

A) 128   B) 170   C) 255   D) 256   E) 511

Problem 16. The line $ax - by = -9$ passes through the points $(-1, 3)$ and $(-3, 0)$. What is the value of $a + b$?

A) 5   B) 6   C) 7   D) 8   E) 9

Problem 17. If $x = \dfrac{\sqrt{13} - 1}{\sqrt{3} + 1}$, then find the value of the expression $\dfrac{\sqrt{3} - 1}{\sqrt{13} + 1}$ in terms of x.

A) $\dfrac{x}{3}$ B) $\dfrac{x}{6}$ C) $\dfrac{x}{9}$ D) $\dfrac{2}{x}$ E) $\dfrac{6}{x}$

Problem 18. N is the number 111...11 formed by writing 105 ones in a row. What is the sum of the digits of the product $105 \times N$?

A) 612   B) 621   C) 630   D) 639   E) 648

Problem 19. In how many ways can three different integers be selected from 1 to 10 such that no two integers chosen are consecutive?

A) 30   B) 56   C) 120   D) 360   E) 720

Problem 20. Suppose ABC is a right triangle with $\overline{AB} \perp \overline{AC}$ and $AB = AC = 20$. A point D is given inside $\triangle ABC$ such that $\overline{AD} \perp \overline{BD}$ and $BD = 16$. What is the area of $\triangle BCD$?

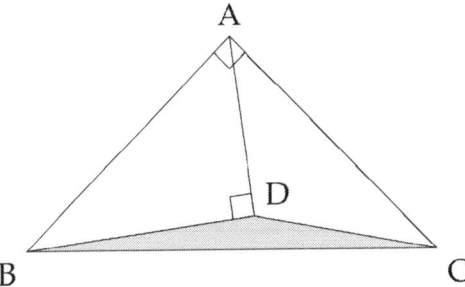

A) 24
B) 28
C) 30
D) 32
E) 36

Practice Exam 5

Problem 21. If $x, y, -\frac{1}{2}$ is an arithmetic progression and $4, x, y$ is a geometric progression, then what is the value of $x + y$?

A) $\frac{6}{5}$ B) $\frac{5}{4}$ C) $\frac{5}{3}$ D) 5   E) None of the preceding

Problem 22. Suppose p is a prime number, x is a positive integer, and n is a non-negative integer. For how many (x, n, p) do we have $n^2 p < 100$ and $n^2 + \frac{50x}{p} = (n + x)^2$?

A) 13   B) 14   C) 15   D) 16   E) 17

Problem 23. A coin is weighted so that it has probability p of landing heads and probability $1-p$ of landing tails, where $0 < p < 1$. If this coin is flipped twice, the probability that two heads are obtained is exactly twice the probability that exactly one head is obtained. What is p?

A) $\frac{1}{2}$ B) $\frac{2}{3}$ C) $\frac{3}{4}$ D) $\frac{4}{5}$ E) $\frac{5}{6}$

Practice Exam 5

Problem 24. ABC is an isosceles triangle with $AB = AC = 5$ and $BC = 8$. Point P is inside $\triangle ABC$ such that the product of the area of $\triangle APB$, the area of $\triangle APC$, and the area of $\triangle BPC$ is maximum. What is the value of PB?

A) 3

B) $\sqrt{10}$

C) $2\sqrt{3}$

D) $\sqrt{17}$

E) $2\sqrt{5}$

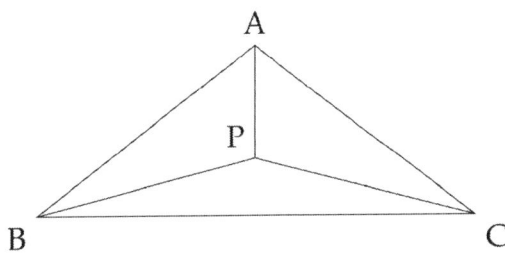

Problem 25. A mathematician offers you the following game. He will flip 10 fair coins, and if n coins land heads, then you win n^2 dollars (for example, if 4 coins land heads, then you win $16, and if 0 coins land heads, then you win $0). How many dollars should the mathematician charge to play the game so that the game is fair?

Note: A game is *fair* if the expected profit after playing the game is zero.

A) $25   B) $27.50   C) $28   D) $28.50   E) $30

Assessment for Practice Exam 5

Q #	Topic	YA	CA	☑ ☒ ☐	Notes
1	Algebra				
2	Number Theory				
3	Combinatorics				
4	Geometry				
5	Algebra				
6	Number Theory				
7	Combinatorics				
8	Geometry				
9	Algebra				
10	Number Theory				
11	Combinatorics				
12	Geometry				
13	Algebra				
14	Number Theory				
15	Combinatorics				
16	Geometry				
17	Algebra				
18	Number Theory				
19	Combinatorics				
20	Geometry				
21	Algebra				
22	Number Theory				
23	Combinatorics				
24	Geometry				
25	Algebra				

CA: Correct Answer   YA: Your Answer   ☑ Correct   ☒ Incorrect   ☐ Empty

Practice Exam 6

- You have **75 minutes** for **25 problems**.

- There are no penalties for incorrect answers. Answer as many problems as you can; return to the others in the time you have left for the test.

Problem 1. The length of a string is x. When two other strings, one of which is twice as long and the other three times as long, are connected to the original string at the right and the left ends respectively, the midpoint of these three strings altogether is 6 feet to the left of the mid-point of the original string. Which is the value of x?

A) 12 feet   B) 15 feet   C) 18 feet   D) 24 feet   E) 32 feet

Problem 2. Suppose x is a positive integer and the number $45 \cdot x$ is made of the digits "0" and "6". What is the sum of all digits of the minimum possible value of x?

A) 9   B) 10   C) 11   D) 12   E) 13

Practice Exam 6

Problem 3. Nine points are equally spaced around the circumference of a circle. How many non-equilateral triangles can be formed by choosing three of these nine points as vertices of the triangle?

    A) 42   B) 72   C) 75   D) 81   E) 84

Problem 4. ABCD is a quadrilateral and E is a point on ABCD such that $\overline{AE}$ and $\overline{DE}$ are angle bisectors of $\angle BAD$ and $\angle ADC$, respectively. What is the value of $m\angle AED$?

A) 60°

B) 75°

C) 90°

D) 100°

E) None of the preceding

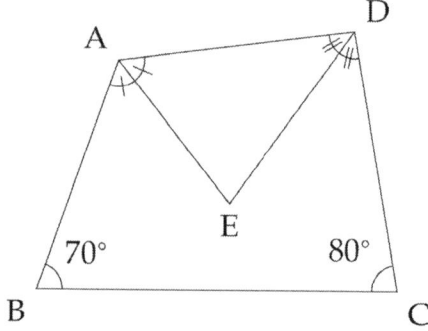

Problem 5. The arithmetic mean of X and Y is 12, the arithmetic mean of X and Z is 6, and the arithmetic mean of Y and Z is 4. What is the value of Z?

    A) −5   B) −2   C) 6   D) 10   E) 12

Practice Exam 6

Problem 6. Suppose a and b are positive integers and $a^2 - b^2$ is a prime number. Which of the following is always correct?

A) $ab = a + b - 1$

B) $ab = a + b + 1$

C) $a^2 - b^2 = 2$

D) $(a - b)^2 = a + b - 2$

E) $a - b = 1$

Problem 7. For numbering the pages of a book, a total of 2933 digits are used. How many pages does this book have?

A) 1010   B) 1001   C) 1105   D) 1110   E) 1015

Problem 8. ABCD is a quadrilateral with $\overline{AB} \perp \overline{AD}$, $m\angle ABC = 45°$, $BC = 5\sqrt{2}$, $AD = 10$, and $AB = 17$. What is the value of CD?

A) $8\sqrt{2}$

B) 12

C) $9\sqrt{2}$

D) 13

E) None of the preceding

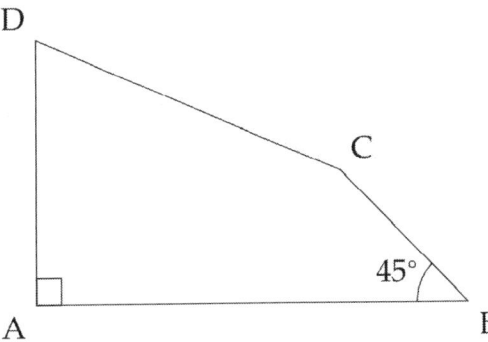

Practice Exam 6

Problem 9. If x and y are positive whole numbers and $x + \dfrac{y^3}{5} = 26$, then what is the value of y?

  A) 2   B) 3   C) 4   D) 5   E) 6

Problem 10. For how many <u>distinct</u> integer values of n is $\dfrac{n^2}{n+4}$ also an integer?

  A) 4   B) 5   C) 8   D) 10   E) 12

Problem 11. There are 5 students in a math team, and 2 chaperones join them at a math competition. They pose for a group photo and sit in 5 chairs arranged in a line. The photographer requests that there be exactly two students between the chaperones. How many ways can they be arranged for the photo?

  A) 120   B) 240   C) 360   D) 480   E) 960

Practice Exam 6

Problem 12. A rectangular sheet of paper is placed on top of another as shown with $AB = 3$, $DE = 2$, $BI = 6$, and $DG = 9$. The dimensions of the larger sheet are double those of the smaller sheet. What is the total shaded area?

A) 96
B) 102
C) 106
D) 110
E) 114

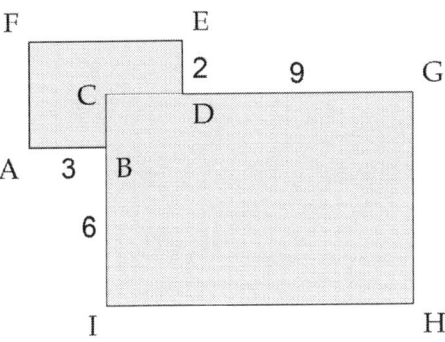

Problem 13. What is the value of n so that $(n + 3^{2019})^2 - (n - 3^{2019})^2 = 3^{2019} + 3^{2020}$?

A) 1
B) 9
C) 3^{2019}
D) 3^{2020}
E) 3^{2038}

Problem 14. How many positive integers not exceeding 2017 are multiples of 3 or 4 but not 5?

A) 792
B) 807
C) 917
D) 927
E) None

Practice Exam 6

Problem 15. In how many ways can 9 different red and 6 different white balls be arranged in a row with no two white balls next to each other?

A) $P(10,9) \cdot 6!$

B) $C(10,9) \cdot 6!$

C) $P(10,6) \cdot 9!$

D) $P(10,9) \cdot 6!$

E) None of the preceding

Problem 16. What is the area of the triangle formed by the lines $y = 6 - x$, $y = 6 + x$, and $y = 2$?

A) 16   B) 18   C) 19   D) 20   E) 21

Problem 17. Patrick, the master gardener, has 100 lbs of tomatoes that were 90% water by weight. He dried the tomatoes in the sun until they were 80% water by weight. How much do Partick's sun-dried tomatoes weigh? Round your answer to the nearest 10 lbs.

A) 50   B) 60   C) 65   D) 70   E) 75

Practice Exam 6

Problem 18. The product of two prime numbers is one less than a perfect square. Given that both prime numbers are less than 100, what is the largest possible value of one of these primes?

A) 73 B) 79 C) 83 D) 89 E) 97

Problem 19. Two cards are dealt from a standard deck of 52 playing cards, without replacement. What is the probability that the cards are of the same suit?

A) $\dfrac{1}{17}$ B) $\dfrac{3}{17}$ C) $\dfrac{4}{17}$ D) $\dfrac{3}{13}$ E) $\dfrac{1}{4}$

Problem 20. $\triangle ABC$ is an isosceles triangle with $AB = AC$ and $m\angle BAC = 120°$. The points F and G are the midpoints of $\overline{AB}$ and $\overline{AC}$ respectively. The points D and E are on $\overline{BC}$ such that $\overline{DF} \perp \overline{AB}$ and $\overline{EG} \perp \overline{AC}$. If $BC = 24$, what is the area of FGED?

A) 20 B) $20\sqrt{3}$ C) 24 D) 32 E) 40

Practice Exam 6

Problem 21. How many pairs (x, y) of real numbers satisfy the following system of equations?

$$x^2 + xy = 2y^2 \quad \text{and} \quad y^2 - xy = 1$$

A) 0   B) 1   C) 2   D) 3   E) None of the preceding

Problem 22. Let $T(n)$ be the digit sum of a positive integer n. For example, $T(5081) = 5 + 0 + 8 + 1 = 14$. How many positive three-digit numbers n satisfy $T(n) + 3n = 2020$?

A) 0   B) 1   C) 2   D) 3   E) 4

Problem 23. As shown in the figure, 12 points are chosen on a 4×7 grid. How many different right triangles can be drawn using these points?

A) 28
B) 29
C) 30
D) 31
E) 32

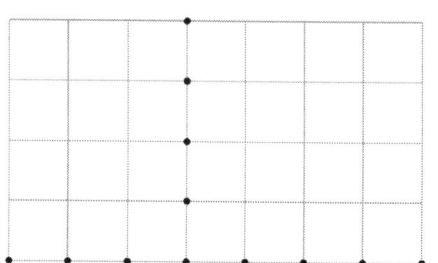

Problem 24. In $\triangle ABC$, the medians $\overline{BE}$ and $\overline{CD}$ intersect at the point G so that $\overline{BE} \perp \overline{CD}$. If $BE = 18$ and $CD = 24$, what is the value of AG?

A) 15   B) 20   C) 25   D) 30   E) None of the preceding

Problem 25. ABCD is a parallelogram. The points E and F are on $\overline{CD}$ and $\overline{BC}$, respectively, such that $BF = FC$ and $CE = 3ED$. The points H and G are such that $\overleftrightarrow{BE} \cap \overrightarrow{AD} = G$ and $\overleftrightarrow{BE} \cap \overleftrightarrow{AF} = H$. If $BH : HE : EG = a : b : c$ for some positive integers a, b and c, what is the minimum value of $a + b + c$?

A) 21
B) 36
C) 40
D) 44
E) 48

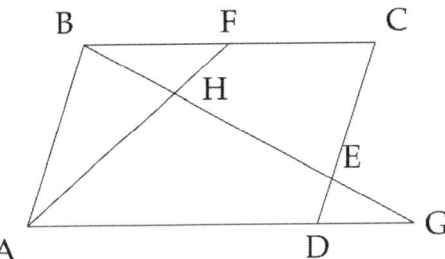

Assessment for Practice Exam 6

Q #	Topic	YA	CA	☑ ☒ ☐	Notes
1	Algebra				
2	Number Theory				
3	Combinatorics				
4	Geometry				
5	Algebra				
6	Number Theory				
7	Combinatorics				
8	Geometry				
9	Algebra				
10	Number Theory				
11	Combinatorics				
12	Geometry				
13	Algebra				
14	Number Theory				
15	Combinatorics				
16	Geometry				
17	Algebra				
18	Number Theory				
19	Combinatorics				
20	Geometry				
21	Algebra				
22	Number Theory				
23	Combinatorics				
24	Geometry				
25	Algebra				

CA: Correct Answer   YA: Your Answer   ☑ Correct   ☒ Incorrect   ☐ Empty

Practice Exam 7

- You have **75 minutes** for **25 problems**.

- There are no penalties for incorrect answers. Answer as many problems as you can; return to the others in the time you have left for the test.

Problem 1. The car with speed 40 mph travels from Arlington Heights to Mt. Prospect and with speed 60 mph from Mt. Prospect to Arlington Heights. Which of the following is the average speed of the car for the entire trip?

    A) 48   B) 49   C) 50   D) 51   E) 52

Problem 2. A 500 page book is numbered consecutively, starting with 1. How many times does the digit 1 appear in the page numbers?

    A) 150   B) 160   C) 180   D) 190   E) 200

Practice Exam 7

Problem 3. Raj rolls a standard 6-sided die. Sena rolls a second 6-sided die. Raj wins if the values shown differ by 1. What is the probability that Sena loses?

A) $\dfrac{1}{3}$ B) $\dfrac{2}{9}$ C) $\dfrac{1}{6}$ D) $\dfrac{5}{18}$ E) $\dfrac{7}{36}$

Problem 4. One side of a triangle has length 6.3 and another side has length 1.7. How many integer values are possible for the length of the third side?

A) 1 B) 2 C) 3 D) 4 E) 5

Problem 5. If $A = \sqrt{\dfrac{1}{16} - \dfrac{1}{25}}$ and $B = \sqrt{\dfrac{1}{16}} - \sqrt{\dfrac{1}{25}}$, then what is the value of $\dfrac{A}{B}$?

A) 1 B) 3 C) 6 D) 8 E) None

Problem 6. How many integers from 2 to 99 inclusive have at least one digit that is a prime number?

A) 72   B) 64   C) 48   D) 36   E) 18

Problem 7. The acute angles of an obtuse triangle measure $a°$ and $b°$. If both of a and b are prime numbers, what is the maximum value of $a + b$?

A) 86   B) 87   C) 88   D) 89   E) None of the preceding

Problem 8. ABC is an isosceles triangle with $AB = BC$. D is a point inside $\triangle ABC$ such that $AD = DC$. If $m\angle ABC = 50°$ and $m\angle ADC = 130°$, what is the value of $m\angle BAD =?$

A) 35°   B) 40°   C) 45°   D) 50°   E) 55°

Practice Exam 7

Problem 9. Half of a stick is divided into 14 equal parts and the other half of the stick is divided into 9 equal parts. The difference between one of the longer parts and one of the shorter parts measures 10 units. What is the total length of the stick?

  A) 252 B) 378 C) 420 D) 500 E) 504

Problem 10. For how many different values of C is 27C4 divisible by 6?

  A) 0 B) 1 C) 2 D) 3 E) 4

Problem 11. How many three-digit numbers are even but have exactly one odd digit?

  A) 100 B) 125 C) 200 D) 225 E) None of the preceding

Problem 12. The sides of a triangle have lengths 7, 14, and c, where c is an integer. For how many values of c is the triangle acute?

A) 2   B) 3   C) 4   D) 5   E) 8

Problem 13. If $5^2 + 5^3 + ... + 5^{20} = M$, then what is the value of $5^2 + 5^3 + ... + 5^{18}$?

A) $M + 19$ B) $M - 5^{21}$ C) $\dfrac{M - 150}{25}$ D) $\dfrac{M - 36}{9}$ E) $\dfrac{M}{25}$

Problem 14. What is the sum of all prime factors of $11^2 + 55^2$?

A) 16   B) 22   C) 23   D) 25   E) 26

Practice Exam 7

Problem 15. Three tiles are marked A and two other tiles are marked B. The five tiles are randomly arranged in a row. What is the probability that the arrangement reads ABABA?

A) $\dfrac{1}{10}$ B) $\dfrac{1}{8}$ C) $\dfrac{1}{6}$ D) $\dfrac{1}{5}$ E) $\dfrac{1}{4}$

Problem 16. How many distinct isosceles triangles can be created with integer sides and a perimeter of 200 units?

A) 49   B) 64   C) 81   D) 96   E) None of the preceding

Problem 17. Mrs. Walker leaves for a walk at 11:00 am starting at point A. She walks from A to B on level ground, walks uphill from B to C, walks downhill from C to D, turns around, and then retraces her steps and returns to point A at 1:00 pm the same day. If her speed is four miles per hour on level ground, three miles per hour uphill, and six miles per hour downhill, how far does she walk in total?

A) 8 miles   B) 9 miles   C) 10 miles   D) 12 miles   E) 16 miles

Practice Exam 7

Problem 18. x and y are positive integers such that $2^8 \cdot 3^2 = x^y$. What is the smallest possible value of x + y?

A) 24 B) 48 C) 50 D) 60 E) 128

Problem 19. How many positive integers smaller than 1000 have exactly 9 positive divisors?

A) 4 B) 6 C) 8 D) 10 E) None of the preceding

Problem 20. As shown in the figure, $\overline{AB}$ is a diameter of a semicircle. C is a point on $\overline{AB}$ with AC = 4. D is a point on the arc AB such that CD = 8 and $\overline{AB} \perp \overline{CD}$. What is the area of the semicircle?

A) 16π
B) 20π
C) 25π
D) 36π
E) 50π

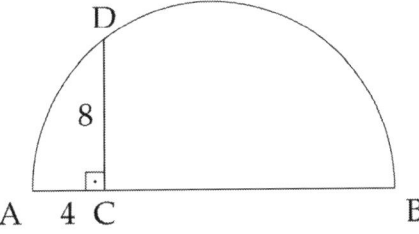

Practice Exam 7

Problem 21. Let a, b and c be positive integers with $a \leq b$. Suppose $x^a + x^b = x^{111c}$ has a positive integer solution x. Which of the following is always correct?

A) $a + b = 111c$

B) $111c = a + 1$

C) $x \geq 111c$

D) c is odd number

E) None of the preceding

Problem 22. For some positive integer n, the sum of two real numbers is n, and the sum of their squares is $n + 19$. What is the possible maximum value of n?

A) 5 B) 6 C) 7 D) 8 E) 9

Problem 23. Ahmad has 12 marbles. In how many ways can he share with Ben and Cannor so that each of the people has at least 1 marble?

A) 45 B) 55 C) 65 D) 105 E) 132

78

Problem 24. What is the area of the right triangle $\triangle ABC$ with side lengths a, b and c, as shown in the figure, satisfying $a + b + c = 28$ and $a^2 + b^2 + c^2 = 288$?

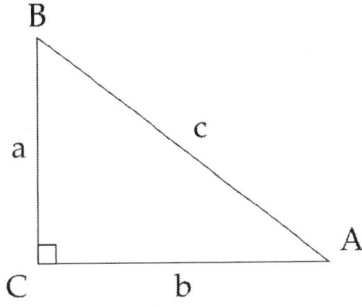

A) 22

B) 24

C) 26

D) 28

E) None of the preceding

Problem 25. What is the minimum value of $x + y + z + t$, where x, y, z and t are positive integers satisfying $3^{8x} + 3^{5y} + 3^{12z} = 3^{19t}$?

A) 148   B) 154   C) 160   D) 166   E) 172

Assessment for Practice Exam 7

Q #	Topic	YA	CA	✓	✗	☐	Notes
1	Algebra						
2	Number Theory						
3	Combinatorics						
4	Geometry						
5	Algebra						
6	Number Theory						
7	Combinatorics						
8	Geometry						
9	Algebra						
10	Number Theory						
11	Combinatorics						
12	Geometry						
13	Algebra						
14	Number Theory						
15	Combinatorics						
16	Geometry						
17	Algebra						
18	Number Theory						
19	Combinatorics						
20	Geometry						
21	Algebra						
22	Number Theory						
23	Combinatorics						
24	Geometry						
25	Algebra						

CA: Correct Answer   YA: Your Answer   ✓ Correct   ✗ Incorrect   ☐ Empty

Practice Exam 8

♦ You have **75 minutes** for **25 problems**.

♦ <u>There are no penalties for incorrect answers</u>. Answer as many problems as you can; return to the others in the time you have left for the test.

Problem 1. If a, b and c are positive integers such that $\frac{a}{b} = 5$ and $\frac{b}{c} = \frac{2}{3}$, then which of the following is the smallest value $a + b + c$ can take?

A) 10 B) 12 C) 14 D) 15 E) 16

Problem 2. On her first day of work, Janabel sold one widget. On day two, she sold three widgets. On day three, she sold five widgets, and on each succeeding day, she sold two more widgets than she had sold on the previous day. How many widgets in total had Janabel sold after working 20 days?

A) 39 B) 99 C) 100 D) 400 E) None of the preceding

Practice Exam 8

Problem 3. How many 4-digit positive integers having only odd digits are divisible by 5?

A) 75   B) 80   C) 100   D) 125   E) 150

Problem 4. Two angles of an isosceles triangle measure 80° and x°. What is the sum of possible values of x°?

A) 60°   B) 70°   C) 80°   D) 90°   E) 150°

Problem 5. If $a + c = 4.98$ and $b + c = 6.48$, what is the value of $b^2 + bc - ab - ca$?

A) 7.47   B) 8.16   C) 9.08   D) 9.72   E) None of the preceding

Practice Exam 8

Problem 6. What is the tens digit of $15! - 10!$?

A) 0 B) 2 C) 5 D) 8 E) 9

Problem 7. What is the probability that a randomly chosen 3-digit number between 200 and 300 is divisible by one of its digits?

A) $\frac{1}{3}$ B) $\frac{23}{33}$ C) $\frac{31}{99}$ D) $\frac{26}{33}$ E) None of the preceding

Problem 8. What is the area of the region bounded by the x-axis, the y-axis, the line $y = 4x+4$, and the line $y = -x + 9$?

A) 24 B) 32 C) 36 D) 38 E) 40

Practice Exam 8

Problem 9. Suppose a and b represent positive numbers. Of the two numbers, a is the smaller and b the larger. What number represents the point two-thirds of the way between a and b on a number line?

A) $\dfrac{a+b}{3}$
B) $\dfrac{a+2b}{3}$
C) $\dfrac{3a+b}{3}$
D) $\dfrac{2a+2b}{3}$
E) None of the preceding

Problem 10. How many positive integer values for n make $n^{18/n}$ an integer?

A) 5
B) 6
C) 7
D) 8
E) None of the preceding

Problem 11. A circle is inscribed in a square of side length of 4. A point X is randomly and uniformly chosen inside the square. What is the probability that X is inside the circle?

A) $\dfrac{\pi}{6}$
B) $\dfrac{\pi}{4}$
C) $\dfrac{2\pi}{3}$
D) $\dfrac{3\pi}{4}$
E) $\dfrac{5\pi}{6}$

Practice Exam 8

Problem 12. △ABC is an isosceles triangle with AB = AC. Point D is on $\overline{BC}$ such that $3m\angle CAD = m\angle BAD$. If $m\angle ADC = 110°$, what is the $m\angle ABC$?

A) 30°
B) 35°
C) 40°
D) 45°
E) 50°

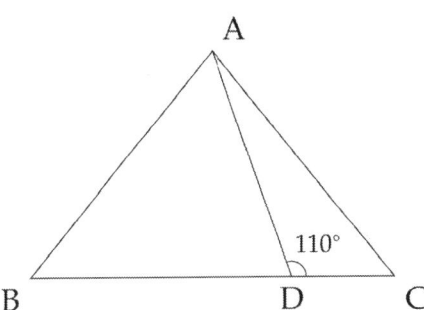

Problem 13. Josh bought 4 lb. of apples, 5 lb. of bananas, and 3 lb. of peaches for $7. Sam bought 2 lb. of apples, 1 lb. of bananas, and 3 lb. of peaches for $5 from the same store. If somebody wants to buy 1 lb. of bananas, 1 lb. of apples, and 1 lb. of peaches, then how much will the total cost be?

A) $3.5   B) $3   C) $2   D) $1.5   E) $1

Problem 14. Both roots of the quadratic equation $x^2 - 19x + k$ are prime numbers. What is the number of possible values of k?

A) 0   B) 1   C) 2   D) 5   E) Infinitely many

Practice Exam 8

Problem 15. A jar contains 3 red and 4 green balls. Two balls are drawn at random without replacement. If the two balls have different colors, what is the probability that the second ball is green?

A) $\frac{1}{2}$ B) $\frac{1}{3}$ C) $\frac{1}{4}$ D) $\frac{1}{5}$ E) None of the preceding

Problem 16. Suppose ABCD is a square with side length 2 units. If a circle tangent to $\overline{AB}$ at E contains C and D, what is the radius of the circle?

A) 1

B) $\frac{5}{4}$

C) $\frac{5}{2}$

D) $\frac{6}{5}$

E) None of the preceding

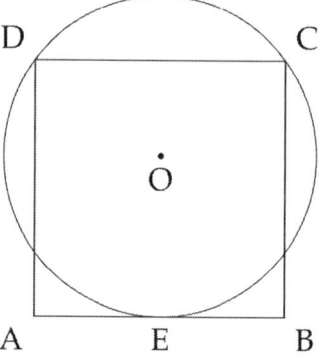

Problem 17. Two different integers a and b satisfy the equation $5^a + 7^b = 6(7b - 5a)$. What is the value of $a + b$?

A) 0 B) 1 C) 2 D) 3 E) 4

Practice Exam 8

Problem 18. Let a, b and c be distinct prime numbers such that $a(c-b) = 18$ and $b(c-a) = 40$. What is the value of $a + b + c$?

A) 13   B) 17   C) 19   D) 21   E) None of the preceding

Problem 19. How many pairs of positive integers (m, n) satisfy $n + m^2 \leq 29$?

A) 30   B) 43   C) 59   D) 85   E) 90

Problem 20. Suppose ABCD is a square with $AB = 30$. If K is the intersection of its diagonals, and L is on $\overline{AB}$ such that $AL = 7$, what is the value of KL?

A) 13
B) 15
C) 17
D) $15\sqrt{2}$
E) None of the preceding

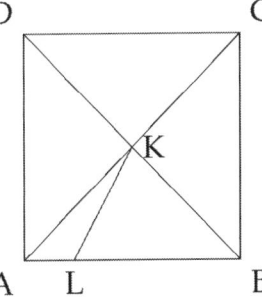

87

Practice Exam 8

Problem 21. Suppose A, B, and C represent digits different than zero such that the sum $AAA + BBB + CCC$ of three-digit numbers equals the four-digit number $ABBC$. Find the value of $A + B + C$.

    A) 14   B) 16   C) 18   D) 23   E) 24

Problem 22. As n ranges over all positive integers, how many distinct values can be found for the greatest common divisor of $6n + 15$ and $10n + 21$?

    A) 2   B) 3   C) 4   D) 5   E) 6

Problem 23. How many ordered pairs of integers (a, b) satisfy the equation $a^4 + b^2 = 4b$?

    A) 2   B) 4   C) 5   D) 6   E) 8

Problem 24. Let P be a point inside of equilateral triangle $\triangle ABC$ such that $m\angle APB = 150°$, $AP = 2\sqrt{3}$ and $BP = 2$. What is the value of PC?

A) 2　　　　B) $2\sqrt{3}$　　　　C) 4　　　　D) $4\sqrt{3}$　　　　E) 6

Problem 25. Suppose $n > 1$ is an integer. For each $k = 1, 2, \ldots, n$, let $d(k)$ be the number of digits in k (e.g., $d(32) = 2, d(708) = 3, d(60093) = 5$, and so on). If

$$d(1) + d(2) + \cdots + d(n) = 2013,$$

find the digit sum of n (e.g., the digit sum of 65003 is $6 + 5 + 0 + 0 + 3 = 14$).

A) 5　　　　B) 14　　　　C) 15　　　　D) 16　　　　E) 19

Assessment for Practice Exam 8

Q #	Topic	YA	CA	☑ ☒ ☐	Notes
1	Algebra				
2	Number Theory				
3	Combinatorics				
4	Geometry				
5	Algebra				
6	Number Theory				
7	Combinatorics				
8	Geometry				
9	Algebra				
10	Number Theory				
11	Combinatorics				
12	Geometry				
13	Algebra				
14	Number Theory				
15	Combinatorics				
16	Geometry				
17	Algebra				
18	Number Theory				
19	Combinatorics				
20	Geometry				
21	Algebra				
22	Number Theory				
23	Combinatorics				
24	Geometry				
25	Algebra				

CA: Correct Answer   YA: Your Answer   ☑ Correct   ☒ Incorrect   ☐ Empty

Practice Exam 9

- You have **75 minutes** for **25 problems**.
- <u>There are no penalties for incorrect answers</u>. Answer as many problems as you can; return to the others in the time you have left for the test.

Problem 1. Suppose $x + \dfrac{1}{y} = 3.125$. Find the decimal equal to $\dfrac{y}{xy+1}$.

A) 0.25 B) 0.32 C) 0.8 D) 1.25 E) 3.35

Problem 2. A four-digit number $53xy$ is divisible by 3, 4, and 5. What is the sum of all possible x values?

A) 4 B) 7 C) 11 D) 12 E) 13

Practice Exam 9

Problem 3. A mathematical game on a computer changes the number displayed on the screen when you press A, B, or C. It adds 3 when you click on A, subtracts 3 when you click on B, and divides by 2 when you click on C. If the number currently displayed is 64, what is the least number of clicks required to get the number 1?

A) 4   B) 5   C) 6   D) 7   E) 8

Problem 4. The lengths, in inches, of the sides of the equilateral triangle are $a + 2b$, $3a - b$, and $5b - a$. Which of the following **could not** be the values of a and b?

A) $(12, 8)$ B) $\left(\frac{9}{2}, 3\right)$ C) $(10, 6)$ D) $(3, 2)$ E) $\left(\frac{3}{2}, 1\right)$

Problem 5. When an empty jar is filled with water, it weighs 6 pounds. When 3/7 of the water is poured out, the jar weighs 4 pounds. How much does the empty jar weigh in pounds?

A) $\frac{4}{3}$ B) $\frac{3}{2}$ C) $\frac{5}{3}$ D) 2   E) $\frac{5}{2}$

Problem 6. What is the largest value for the length of a list of consecutive integers whose sum is 55?

A) 10   B) 25   C) 55   D) 110   E) 135

Problem 7. You have six sticks of the following lengths: 1 cm, 2 cm, 3 cm, 11 cm, 12 cm, and 13 cm. You have to choose three of these sticks to form a triangle. How many different choices of three sticks are there that work?

A) 4   B) 5   C) 6   D) 7   E) 8

Problem 8. Two lines which intersect at $(2,2)$ have slopes -2 and $\frac{1}{2}$. What is the area of the triangle enclosed by these two lines and the line $x = 0$?

A) 4   B) 8   C) 10   D) 12   E) None of the preceding

Practice Exam 9

Problem 9. In the table the sum of the entries in each column, row, and diagonal is equal to 42. What is the value of c?

A) 6
B) 8
C) 10
D) 12
E) 14

c		
	$2x + 2$	x
12		20

Problem 10. Which of the following is equal to the sum of primes p such that $p^2 + 11$ has exactly 9 positive divisors? (Include 1 and the number itself.)

A) 2   B) 3   C) 5   D) 7   E) More than 7

Problem 11. How many three digit numbers have digits whose product is 12?

A) 3   B) 6   C) 9   D) 12   E) 15

94

Practice Exam 9

Problem 12. The two legs of a right triangle, which are altitudes, have lengths $4\sqrt{3}$ and 12. How long is the third altitude of the triangle?

A) 2   B) 4   C) 5   D) 6   E) 8

Problem 13. Based on the pattern, find how many more shaded squares than unshaded squares will be in the 50th diagram in the sequence.

A) 50
B) 60
C) 80
D) 100
E) 150

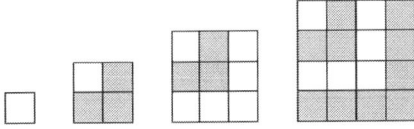

Problem 14. Suppose abcd and badc are four-digit numbers. If $abcd - badc = 1818$, then find $(a - b) + (d - c)$.

A) 0   B) 2   C) 4   D) 6   E) None of the preceding

Practice Exam 9

Problem 15. A triple (x, y, z) of integers with $x, y, z \geq 0$ is chosen at random such that $2x + y + z = 4$. What is the probability that $x + y + z = 3$?

A) $\dfrac{4}{9}$ B) $\dfrac{5}{9}$ C) $\dfrac{11}{18}$ D) $\dfrac{2}{3}$ E) None of the preceding

Problem 16. $\triangle ABC$ is a triangle with $AC = 12$. The bisector of $\angle A$ meets $\overline{BC}$ at D, and $CD = 4$. The set of all possible values of AB is an open interval (a, b). What is $a + b$?

A) 20   B) 24   C) 28   D) 30   E) 32

Problem 17. Suppose $a, b,$ and c are positive integers such that $a + \dfrac{1}{b + \dfrac{1}{c+1}} = \dfrac{23}{7}$. Find $2a + b + c$.

A) 7   B) 8   C) 9   D) 10   E) None of the preceding

Problem 18. How many integer pairs (m, n) satisfy the equation $m \cdot n + n + 14 = (m-1)^2$?

A) 2   B) 6   C) 8   D) 10   E) 12

Problem 19. How many four-digit positive integers can be found so that all four digits are prime numbers and the sum of the digits is even?

A) 172   B) 168   C) 150   D) 144   E) 136

Problem 20. ABCD is a trapezoid with $\overline{AD} \parallel \overline{BC}$, $\overline{AB} \perp \overline{AD}$, AB = 8, AD = 6 and DC = EC = 10. What is the area of ABDE?

A) 28
B) 32
C) 36
D) 40
E) None of the preceding

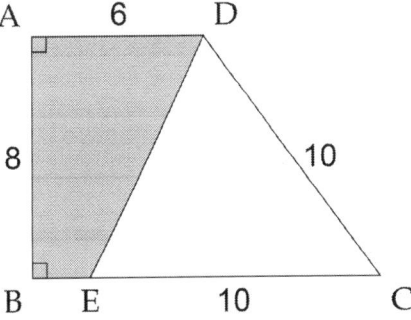

Practice Exam 9

Problem 21. The real number $\sqrt{19 - 8\sqrt{3}}$ can be expressed in the form $a + b\sqrt{3}$ where a and b are integers and a is positive. What is the value of $a + b$?

A) 3 B) 4 C) 6 D) 7 E) 8

Problem 22. An EZ number is defined as any positive integer with the following properties: i) It has at least two digits, ii) All its digits are the same, and iii) It has exactly 4 positive divisors. For example, $111 = 3 \times 37$ is an EZ number. How many EZ numbers less than 10^5 are there?

A) 7 B) 17 C) 27 D) 37 E) None of the preceding

Problem 23. In a local soccer league with 5 teams, one team plays a total of 20 games. For example, Team A plays with the other 4 teams a total of five times. For each team the below table shows the number of W (Win)- L (Lost)- T- (Tie). What is $x + y - z$?

A) 12
B) 13
C) 14
D) 15
E) None of the preceding

Team	W	L	T
A	2	15	3
B	7	9	4
C	6	12	2
D	10	8	2
E	x	y	z

Problem 24. Suppose ABCD is a trapezoid such that AB ∥ CD, AD = 8, DC = 11, BC = 15, and m∠C + m∠D = 270°. What is the value of AB?

A) 26
B) 28
C) 30
D) 32
E) 34

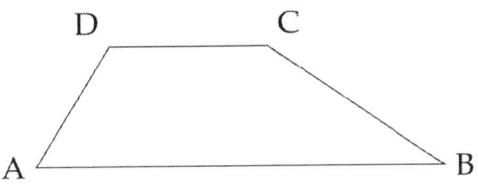

Problem 25. Suppose n is a positive integer. If 2019 digits are used to enumerate the positive integers less than n, what is the digit sum of n?

A) 610 B) 660 C) 710 D) 760 E) None of the preceding

Assessment for Practice Exam 9

Q #	Topic	YA	CA	☑ ☒ ☐	Notes
1	Algebra				
2	Number Theory				
3	Combinatorics				
4	Geometry				
5	Algebra				
6	Number Theory				
7	Combinatorics				
8	Geometry				
9	Algebra				
10	Number Theory				
11	Combinatorics				
12	Geometry				
13	Algebra				
14	Number Theory				
15	Combinatorics				
16	Geometry				
17	Algebra				
18	Number Theory				
19	Combinatorics				
20	Geometry				
21	Algebra				
22	Number Theory				
23	Combinatorics				
24	Geometry				
25	Algebra				

CA: Correct Answer   YA: Your Answer   ☑ Correct   ☒ Incorrect   ☐ Empty

Practice Exam 10

- You have **75 minutes** for **25 problems**.

- There are no penalties for incorrect answers. Answer as many problems as you can; return to the others in the time you have left for the test.

Problem 1. What is 20% of $5^{32} - 5^{30}$?

A) $6 \cdot 5^{28}$ B) $8 \cdot 5^{30}$ C) $24 \cdot 5^{29}$ D) $12 \cdot 5^{29}$ E) $24 \cdot 5^{28}$

Problem 2. If $N = 2018^2 + 4 \cdot 2018 + 4$, then what is the sum of the distinct prime factors of N?

A) 14   B) 17   C) 108   D) 2017   E) 2011

Practice Exam 10

Problem 3. In a mathematics contest with ten problems, a student gains 5 points for a correct answer and loses 2 points for an incorrect answer. If Olivia answered every problem and her score was 29, how many correct answers did she have?

A) 3 B) 4 C) 5 D) 6 E) 7

Problem 4. A square has side length x. To make a new square, the side lengths are increased by 1. The difference between the areas of two squares is 101. What is the value of x?

A) 31 B) 40 C) 45 D) 49 E) 50

Problem 5. Find the value of x for which $100^x \cdot 1000^{2x} = 10000^{10}$.

A) 3 B) 4 C) 5 D) 6 E) 7

Practice Exam 10

Problem 6. If $1! \cdot 2! \cdot 3! \cdots 10! \cdot k$ is a perfect square, what is the minimum value of k?

    A) 5   B) 7   C) 15   D) 21   E) 35

Problem 7. A fair tetrahedral die, whose faces are numbered 1, 2, 3 and 4 is rolled three times. What is the probability that the sum of the numbers rolled is 8?

    A) $\dfrac{3}{16}$ B) $\dfrac{3}{32}$ C) $\dfrac{13}{32}$ D) $\dfrac{23}{32}$ E) None of the preceding

Problem 8. The area of each face of cube A is 8 units^2. The volume of cube B is 75% less than the volume of cube A. What is the volume of cube B in unit^3?

A) $4\sqrt{2}$

B) $\dfrac{8}{3}$

C) $12\sqrt{2}$

D) $\dfrac{\sqrt{2}}{2}$

E) None of the preceding

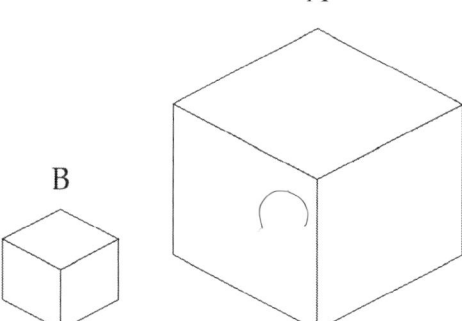

Practice Exam 10

Problem 9. Suppose a and b are non-zero real numbers such that $ax + by = a^2 - ab + b^2$ and $ax - by = a^2 - b^2$. What is the value of $x + y$?

A) $a + \dfrac{b}{4}$ 　　 B) $b + \dfrac{a}{4}$ 　　 C) $b + \dfrac{a}{2}$ 　　 D) $a + \dfrac{b}{3}$ 　　 E) $\dfrac{a+b}{2}$

Problem 10. For how many positive integer values of x is the expression $\dfrac{x^2 - 7x + 60}{x}$ an integer?

A) 24 　　 B) 16 　　 C) 12 　　 D) 10 　　 E) 8

Problem 11. Starting with K, the word KEEP can be formed by moving either horizontally, vertically, or diagonally from square to square in the grid. How many different paths can be followed to form KEEP?

A) 64
B) 72
C) 80
D) 88
E) 96

P	P	P	P	P
P	E	E	E	P
P	E	K	E	P
P	E	E	E	P
P	P	P	P	P

Practice Exam 10

Problem 12. How many of the following five shapes could be the shape of the region where two triangles overlap?

    I. equilateral triangle   II. regular pentagon   III. regular hexagon

                        IV. square   V. kite

A) 1   B) 2   C) 3   D) 4   E) 5

Problem 13. Let A, B and C be three digits so that the sum of the two-digit numbers AB, BC and CA equals the three-digit number ABC. What is $A + B + C$?

A) 12   B) 18   C) 19   D) 20   E) 23

Problem 14. How many perfect cubes lie between $2^9 + 1$ and $2^{15} + 1$, inclusive?

A) 20   B) 24   C) 26   D) 28   E) 31

Practice Exam 10

Problem 15. Suppose a, b, and c are positive integers such that $a + 9b + 15c = 55$. Find the total number of (a, b, c) triples.

A) 3 B) 4 C) 6 D) 7 E) 8

Problem 16. A circle with center O is tangent to $\triangle ABC$ at K, L, and M. If $AM = 8$, $AB = 11$, and $BC = 10$, what is the area of $\triangle ABC$?

A) $12\sqrt{21}$

B) $12\sqrt{3}$

C) $9\sqrt{6}$

D) 24

E) None of the preceding

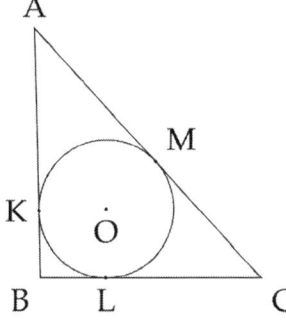

Problem 17. x and y are two numbers such that $y < |y| < x$. What is the simplified version of $|x + y| - |x| + |y|$?

A) 0 B) $2x + 2y$ C) $2x$ D) $2y$ E) $2x - 2y$

Practice Exam 10

Problem 18. Let $O(n)$ denote the sum of the odd digits of n. For example, $O(2019) = 1+9 = 10$. What is $O(1) + O(2) + O(3) + ... + O(98) + O(99)$?

A) 300 B) 350 C) 400 D) 450 E) 500

Problem 19. Three standard six-sided dice are rolled, and the sum S is calculated. What is the probability that $S(21 - S) < 80$?

A) $\dfrac{1}{27}$ B) $\dfrac{5}{81}$ C) $\dfrac{13}{216}$ D) $\dfrac{1}{9}$ E) None of the preceding

Problem 20. ABC is a triangle with $AB = AD = BE$. $m\angle A = 114°$ and $m\angle B = 60°$. Find $m\angle EDC$.

A) 112°
B) 117°
C) 122°
D) 127°
E) 150°

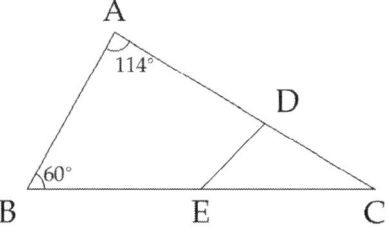

Practice Exam 10

Problem 21. How many real number solutions does the equation $5^x x^2 + 125 = 5^{x+2} + 5x^2$ have?

A) 0   B) 1   C) 3   D) 5   E) Infinitely Many

Problem 22. Numbers of the form $2020a + b$ such that a and b are integers with $1 \leq a < b \leq 2019$ and $b^2 - a^2$ is divisible by 673 are written in increasing order as thus:

$1 \cdot 2020 + 672 = 2692, \quad 1 \cdot 2020 + 674 = 2694, \quad 1 \cdot 2020 + 1345 = 3365, \quad 1 \cdot 2020 + 1347 = 3367, \ldots$

What is the 2020-th number in the sequence?

A) $405 \cdot 2019$ B) $422 \cdot 2019$ C) $506 \cdot 2019$ D) $1011 \cdot 2019$ E) None of the preceding

Problem 23. All positive integers whose digits are all even are written in increasing order in the base ten system. 2, 4, 6, 8, 20, 22, 24, 26, 28, 40, 42, 44, 46, 48, 60, ... Find the 499th number of this pattern.

A) 4444   B) 4666   C) 4888   D) 6666   E) 6888

Problem 24. In a semicircle with center O, m∠OAC = 52° and AC = CD = CE. What is m∠DCE?

A) 24°
B) 28°
C) 32°
D) 36°
E) 40°

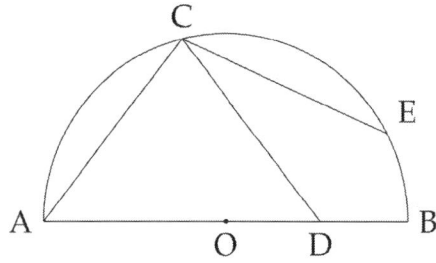

Problem 25. Suppose x and y are real numbers that satisfy $2x^2 - 3y = -\frac{17}{2}$ and $y^2 - 4x = 7$. What is the value of $x + y$?

A) $\frac{7}{2}$
B) $\frac{5}{4}$
C) $\frac{3}{2}$
D) $\frac{1}{4}$
E) None of the preceding

Assessment for Practice Exam 10

Q #	Topic	YA	CA	☑	☒	☐	Notes
1	Algebra						
2	Number Theory						
3	Combinatorics						
4	Geometry						
5	Algebra						
6	Number Theory						
7	Combinatorics						
8	Geometry						
9	Algebra						
10	Number Theory						
11	Combinatorics						
12	Geometry						
13	Algebra						
14	Number Theory						
15	Combinatorics						
16	Geometry						
17	Algebra						
18	Number Theory						
19	Combinatorics						
20	Geometry						
21	Algebra						
22	Number Theory						
23	Combinatorics						
24	Geometry						
25	Algebra						

CA: Correct Answer   YA: Your Answer   ☑ Correct   ☒ Incorrect   ☐ Empty

Solutions

Solutions for Practice Exam 1

Problem 1. In the diagram, each of the five boxes is to contain a number. Each of the three numbers in the three middle boxes (including 28) is equal to the average of the number to its left and the number to its right. What number must occupy the box labeled e?

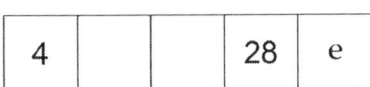

A) 32 B) 34 C) 36 D) 38 E) None of the preceding

Solution. Let the numbers in the empty boxes be x and y as shown in the following figure:

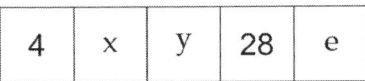

Since each of the numbers in the middle boxes is the average of the numbers in two adjacent boxes, we have
$$x = \frac{4+y}{2}, \quad y = \frac{x+28}{2}, \quad 28 = \frac{y+e}{2}.$$
In other words,
$$2x - y = 4, \quad 2y - x = 28, \quad y + e = 56.$$
We can obtain y from the first two equations:
$$y = \frac{(2x-y) + 2(2y-x)}{3} = \frac{4 + 2 \cdot 28}{3} = 20.$$
We can now obtain e from the last equation:
$$e = (y+e) - y = 56 - 20 = 36.$$
The answer is $\boxed{C}$. □

Problem 2. If a is an even positive integer and b is an odd positive integer, which of the following could represent an odd integer?

A) $a \cdot b$ B) $a + 2b$ C) $a^b + 1$ D) $a + b + 1$ E) $a - b + 1$

Solution. Since a is even and b is odd, suppose $a = 2k$ and $b = 2m + 1$ for some positive integer k and a non-negative integer m. Then

$$ab = (2k)(2m+1) = 2(2km + k) \qquad \text{(even)}$$
$$a + 2b = 2k + 2(2m+1) = 2(k + 2m + 1) \qquad \text{(even)}$$
$$a^b + 1 = (2k)^{2m+1} + 1 = 2(2^{2m} \cdot k^{2m+1}) + 1 \qquad \text{(odd)}$$
$$a + b + 1 = 2k + 2m + 1 + 1 = 2(k + m + 1) \qquad \text{(even)}$$
$$a - b + 1 = 2k - (2m+1) + 1 = 2(k - m) \qquad \text{(even)}$$

The answer is $\boxed{C}$. □

Solutions for Practice Exam 1

Problem 3. A cube of edge length 4 cm is painted green on all faces. It is then cut into 64 identical unit cubes. How many unit cubes have paint on exactly two faces?

    A) 24   B) 28   C) 32   D) 36   E) None of the preceding

Solution. Of the four unit cubes that are along each edge of the big cube, we count the two that are not at the corners. Since the big cube has twelve edges, there are $12 \cdot 2 = 24$ unit cubes with two painted sides. The answer is $\boxed{A}$. □

Problem 4. How many different isosceles triangles have integer side lengths and perimeter 17?

    A) 3   B) 4   C) 5   D) 6   E) 8

Solution. Consider an isosceles triangle with integer side lengths x, x and y and perimeter $2x + y = 17$. Since $2x > y$ by the triangle inequality, we have $17 = 2x + y > 2y$, and so, $17/2 > y$. Then, the possible integer triples (x, x, y) are $(5,5,7)$, $(6,6,5)$, $(7,7,3)$ and $(8,8,1)$. The answer is $\boxed{B}$. □

Problem 5. In the addition problem below, the letters A and B represent different digits. What is the value of $A + B$?

A) 12
B) 13
C) 14
D) 15
E) 16

$$\begin{array}{r} 7\ 7\ B \\ 5\ A\ B \\ +\ A\ A\ B \\ \hline 1\ 8\ B\ 7 \end{array}$$

Solution. The units digit 7 of the sum 18B7 must equal the units digit of $B+B+B = 3 \cdot B$, which is only possible if $3B = 27$. Then $B = 9$ and so, carrying the 2, the units digit of $2+7+A+A = 9+2A$ must be $B = 9$, which implies that $A = 0$ or $A = 5$. Examining the hundreds digit of the sum 18B7, note that $A \neq 0$ since $7 + 5 + 0 \neq 18$. Hence, $A = 5$ and therefore $A + B = 5 + 9 = 14$. The answer is $\boxed{C}$. □

Problem 6. An integer N has 10 positive divisors. If 2N has 15 positive divisors and 3N has 20 positive divisors, how many positive divisors does 4N have?

    A) 12   B) 20   C) 30   D) 36   E) 40

Solutions for Practice Exam 1

Solution. Since the number of positive divisors of N can be represented as either 10 or $2 \cdot 5$, the integer N is represented as

$$N = p^9 \quad \text{or} \quad N = p \cdot q^4$$

for some distinct primes p and q. Hence,

$$2N = \begin{cases} 2 \cdot p^9 & \text{if } p \neq 2, \\ 2^{10} & \text{if } p = 2, \end{cases} \quad \text{or} \quad 2N = \begin{cases} 2 \cdot p \cdot q^4 & \text{if } p, q \neq 2, \\ 2^2 \cdot q^4 & \text{if } p = 2 \text{ and } q \neq 2, \\ p \cdot 2^5 & \text{if } p \neq 2 \text{ and } q = 2. \end{cases}$$

Among those representations, only $2N = 2^2 \cdot q^4$ has 15 positive divisors. Therefore $N = 2 \cdot q^4$, $q \geq 3$, and hence

$$3N = \begin{cases} 2 \cdot 3 \cdot q^4 & \text{if } q > 3, \\ 2 \cdot 3^5 & \text{if } q = 3. \end{cases}$$

The only possible representation for 3N which has 20 positive divisors is $3N = 2 \cdot 3 \cdot q^4$ when $q > 3$. Finally, $4N = 2^3 \cdot q^4$ has 20 positive divisors. The answer is $\boxed{B}$. □

Problem 7. The points in the 3×3 grid below are equally spaced horizontally and vertically. How many squares of any size can be formed by connecting four of the points?

A) 14

B) 15

C) 18

D) 20

E) 21

Solution. The number of 1×1 squares is 9. The number of 2×2 squares is 4. The number of 3×3 squares is 1. The number of $\sqrt{2} \times \sqrt{2}$ squares is 4. The number of $\sqrt{5} \times \sqrt{5}$ squares is 2. Therefore, there are 20 squares in total. The answer is $\boxed{D}$. □

Problem 8. In a convex pentagon ABCDE, $m\angle A = 40°$, $m\angle B = m\angle E$ and $m\angle C = m\angle D$. What is the sum of the measures of $\angle B$ and $\angle C$?

A) 225°   B) 230°   C) 240°   D) 250°   E) Cannot be determined

Solution. Let $m\angle B = m\angle E = x$ and $m\angle C = m\angle D = y$. Since the sum of the internal angles in a convex pentagon is 540°, we have $2x + 2y + 40° = 540°$. Then $x + y = 250°$. The answer is $\boxed{D}$. □

Solutions for Practice Exam 1

Problem 9. A *magic* number represents the number of dots in a rectangle containing two more rows than columns. The first four magic numbers are 3, 8, 15, and 24. What is the 20th magic number?

A) 341

B) 360

C) 399

D) 440

E) 489

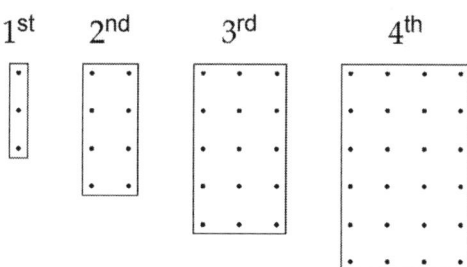

Solution. Notice that there are $n \cdot (n+2)$ dots in the nth shape. Thus, the 20th magic number is $20 \cdot 22 = 440$. The answer is $\boxed{D}$. □

Problem 10. What is the units digit of $2^{2020} \cdot 7^{2020}$?

A) 2   B) 4   C) 6   D) 8   E) 9

Solution. Notice that $2^{2020} \cdot 7^{2020}$ is even. Therefore, the units digit is either $0, 2, 4, 6$ or 8. Then it is enough to compute $(2^{2020} \cdot 7^{2020}) \mod 5$ to obtain the exact units digit. Since $7 \equiv 2 \pmod{5}$, we have

$$(2^{2020} \cdot 7^{2020}) \equiv (2^{2020} \cdot 2^{2020}) \equiv 2^{4040} \pmod{5}.$$

Since $2^4 \equiv 1 \pmod{5}$, we have

$$2^{4040} \equiv (2^4)^{1010} \equiv 1^{1010} \equiv 1 \pmod{5}.$$

Thus, the units digit is 6. The answer is $\boxed{C}$. □

Problem 11. Two brothers and two sisters stand side-by-side for a photograph. The two sisters refuse to stand next to each other. How many different ways can they be arranged for the photo?

A) 12   B) 15   C) 16   D) 18   E) 24

Solution. There are $4! = 24$ ways to arrange four people without any restriction. On the other hand, the number of arrangements such that two sisters are next to each other is $3! \cdot 2! = 12$. Then the result is $24 - 12 = 12$. The answer is $\boxed{A}$. □

Problem 12. Point O is the center of the semicircle where $OD = DB$, $AB \perp CD$, $CD = 2\sqrt{3}$ and $m\angle CAB = 30°$. What is the radius of the circle?

116

Solutions for Practice Exam 1

A) 4
B) $3\sqrt{2}$
C) 5
D) $3\sqrt{3}$
E) 6

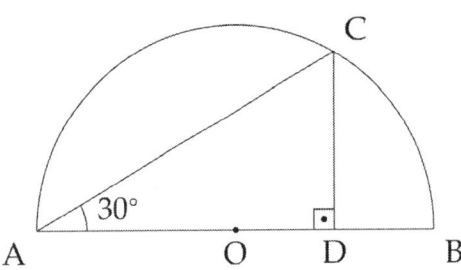

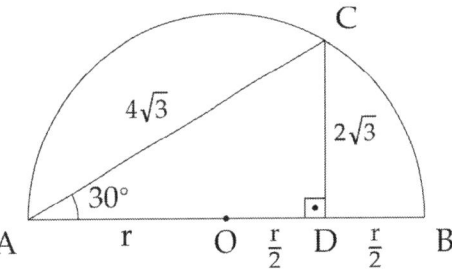

Solution. Let r be the radius of the circle. Then $OD = DB = \frac{r}{2}$. Consider the 30-60-90 right triangle ACD. Then $r + \frac{r}{2} = 2\sqrt{3} \cdot \sqrt{3} = 6$. Thus, $r = 4$. The answer is $\boxed{A}$. □

Problem 13. An 8×10 rectangle is made of 1×1 squares. How many 1×1 squares are needed to represent 0.725 times the area of the whole rectangle?

A) 56
B) 58
C) 60
D) 62
E) 64

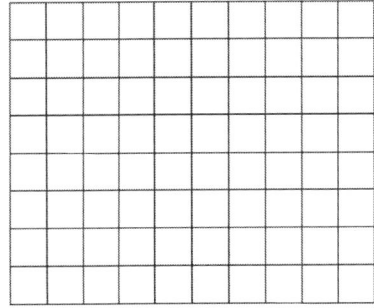

Solution. There are 80 squares in an 8×10 rectangle. Then $0.725 \cdot 80 = 58$ squares are needed. The answer is $\boxed{B}$. □

Problem 14. Robert writes down a list of whole numbers beginning with 1. To generate the next number in the list, he either adds 6 to the previous number, or he multiplies the previous number by 4. For example, his list could be the sequence 1, 7, 28, 34, 40, 160, ...Which of the following numbers *cannot* appear in Robert's sequence?

A) 109 B) 151 C) 244 D) 335 E) 412

Solution. Notice that every number in the sequence has remainder 1 when it is divided by 3. Among the given numbers, only 335 does not have remainder 1. The numbers 109 and 151 appear in the sequence 1, 7, 13, 19, ... On the other hand, the numbers 244 and 412 appear in the sequence 1, 4, 10, 16, 22, ... The answer is $\boxed{D}$. □

Solutions for Practice Exam 1

Problem 15. In a regular octagon, all diagonals are drawn. If a diagonal is chosen at random, what is the probability that it is either one of the shortest or one of the longest?

A) $\dfrac{2}{5}$ B) $\dfrac{3}{5}$ C) $\dfrac{12}{25}$ D) $\dfrac{4}{5}$ E) None of the preceding

Solution. Enumerate the vertices in a clockwise manner by 1, 2, ..., 8 and denote the diagonal joined by the vertices x and y (such that x < y) as {x, y}. Notice that there are 20 diagonals in a regular octagon. The shortest diagonals are {1,3}, {1,7}, {2,4}, {2,8}, {3,5}, {4,6}, {5,7} and {6,8}. The longest diagonals are {1,5}, {2,6}, {3,7} and {4,8}. Therefore, the probability that a randomly chosen diagonal is either one of the shortest or the longest diagonals is $\dfrac{12}{20} = \dfrac{3}{5}$. The answer is $\boxed{B}$.

Problem 16. Two identical regular hexagons are drawn in a rectangle as given in the figure. If the area of each hexagon is 6 in², what is the area of the rectangle?

A) 18 in²
B) 21 in²
C) 24 in²
D) 27 in²
E) None of the preceding

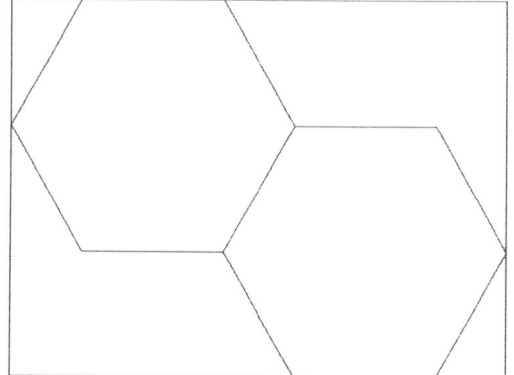

Solution. Refer to the figure. The area of each hexagon is $12A = 6$ in² Therefore, $A = 1/2$ in², and thus the area of the rectangle is $42A = 21$ in². The answer is $\boxed{B}$.

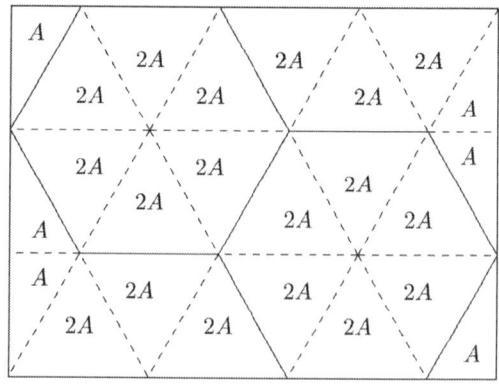

Problem 17. Alfred, Benjamin, and Carl have a total of 252 trading cards. Alfred gives one-fifth of his cards to Benjamin. Benjamin then gives some of his cards to Carl. After this process, all three people have the same number of cards, and Carl has twice as many cards as he had originally. How many cards did Benjamin have originally?

Solutions for Practice Exam 1

A) 42   B) 70   C) 84   D) 105   E) 147

Solution. In the beginning, suppose Alfred and Benjamin have a and b cards, respectively, so Carl has 252 − (a + b) cards. After Alfred gives one-fifth of his cards to Benjamin, Alfred has 4a/5 cards and Benjamin has b + a/5 cards. If Benjamin gives c cards to Carl, so that Benjamin has b + a/5 − c cards and Carl has 252 − (a + b) + c cards, then

$$\frac{4a}{5} = b + \frac{a}{5} - c = 252 - (a+b) + c = 2 \cdot (252 - (a+b)).$$

We have c = 252 − a − b from the last equality. Then,

$$\frac{4a}{5} = b + \frac{a}{5} - c = 2c.$$

Thus, $a = b = \frac{5c}{2}$. Using the fact that c = 252 − a − b = 252 − 5c, we have c = 42. Thus, a = b = 105. The answer is $\boxed{D}$. □

Problem 18. What is the sum of all integers x which make the expression $\frac{2002}{2x-7}$ an integer?

A) −51   B) −32   C) 56   D) 51   E) 0

Solution. Notice that the integer 2x − 7 is odd, and the given expression is an integer only if (2x − 7) is an odd divisor of 2002. Since 2002 = 2 · 7 · 11 · 13, there are 16 odd divisors of 2002:

$$\pm 1, \quad \pm 7, \quad \pm 11, \quad \pm 13, \quad \pm 77, \quad \pm 91, \quad \pm 143, \quad \pm 1001.$$

Since 2x − 7 = ±a has solution $x = \frac{7 \pm a}{2}$, all possible values for x are

$$\frac{7 \pm 1}{2}, \quad \frac{7 \pm 7}{2}, \quad \frac{7 \pm 11}{2}, \quad \frac{7 \pm 13}{2}, \quad \frac{7 \pm 77}{2}, \quad \frac{7 \pm 91}{2}, \quad \frac{7 \pm 143}{2}, \quad \frac{7 \pm 1001}{2}.$$

Notice that a and −a will cancel each other when we add them up. Therefore, the sum of all possible x values are $16 \cdot \frac{7}{2} = 56$. The answer is $\boxed{C}$. □

Problem 19. A doughnut shop offers four flavors of doughnuts: glazed, chocolate, strawberry, and cinnamon. Albert wishes to buy 12 doughnuts, including at least one doughnut of each flavor. How many possible combinations of donuts can Albert buy? (For example, Albert may buy 2 glazed, 5 chocolate, 3 strawberry, and 2 cinnamon doughnuts.)

A) 165   B) 220   C) 286   D) 330   E) 455

Solution. Suppose Albert chooses a glazed, b chocolate, c strawberry and d cinnamon doughnuts. That is, we are looking for positive integer solutions to a + b + c + d = 12. The number of such solutions is C(12 − 1, 4 − 1) = C(11, 3) = 165. The answer is $\boxed{A}$. □

Solutions for Practice Exam 1

Problem 20. The area of the triangle formed by the x-axis, y-axis, and the line $2y = mx + 6$ is 36. What is $|m|$?

A) $\dfrac{1}{16}$ B) $\dfrac{1}{8}$ C) $\dfrac{1}{4}$ D) $\dfrac{3}{4}$ E) $\dfrac{4}{3}$

Solution. The x- and y-intercepts of the line $2y = mx + 6$ are $-\dfrac{6}{m}$ and 3, respectively. Since the area of the triangle is 36, we have

$$36 = \frac{1}{2} \cdot \left(3 \cdot \frac{6}{|m|}\right) = \frac{9}{|m|}.$$

Therefore, $|m| = \dfrac{1}{4}$. The answer is $\boxed{C}$. □

Problem 21. If x and y are real numbers so that $4x^2 + y^4 - 4y^2 - 20x + 29 = 0$, then what is the value of $y^2 + 2x$?

A) 5 B) 7 C) 9 D) 15 E) 29

Solution. Note that

$$0 = 4x^2 + y^4 - 4y^2 - 20x + 29 = (y^2 - 2)^2 + (2x - 5)^2.$$

Since the only solution to $a^2 + b^2 = 0$ is $a = b = 0$, we have $y^2 = 2$ and $2x = 5$. Thus, $y^2 + 2x = 2 + 5 = 7$. The answer is $\boxed{B}$. □

Problem 22. Suppose xx, yy and zz are two-digit whole numbers. If $x^2 + y^2 + z^2 = 74$ then find the number of positive divisors of $(xx)^2 + (yy)^2 + (zz)^2$.

A) 6 B) 8 C) 10 D) 12 E) None of the preceding

Solution. Notice that

$$(xx)^2 + (yy)^2 + (zz)^2 = 11^2(x^2 + y^2 + z^2) = 11^2 \cdot 74 = 2 \cdot 11^2 \cdot 37.$$

Therefore, there are 12 positive divisors. The answer is $\boxed{D}$. □

Problem 23. In how many ways can a blank 3×3 grid be filled with the integers from 1 to 9 so that squares containing consecutive integers are adjacent (i.e., have a common edge)? Hint: Of the three examples below, **A** and **B** satisfy the given conditions, while **C** does not because the squares containing 1 and 2 are not adjacent!

Solutions for Practice Exam 1

A) 28
B) 32
C) 36
D) 40
E) None of the preceding

9	8	7
2	1	6
3	4	5

A

7	8	9
6	5	4
1	2	3

B

1	3	2
6	5	4
7	8	9

C

Solution. We do casework based on the location of the 1.

If the 1 is in the center cell, then the 2 can be in any of the four cells adjacent to 1, and the 3 can be in either of the two cells adjacent to the 2. This uniquely determines the rest of the grid, giving $4 \times 2 = 8$ ways.

If the 1 is in any of the four corner cells, there are 4 ways to choose the location of the 1. Without loss of generality, suppose the 1 is in the upper left cell. There are two possible locations for the 2; suppose the 2 is in the upper cell, as shown:

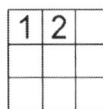

The 3 must go in either the top right cell or the center cell. We enumerate all possibilities:

1	2	3
8	7	4
9	6	5

1	2	3
8	9	4
7	6	5

1	2	3
6	5	4
7	8	9

1	2	9
4	3	8
5	6	7

Hence for any of the $4 \times 2 = 8$ ways to insert 1 and 2 (where 1 is in a corner cell), there are 4 possible grids, giving $4 \times 2 \times 4 = 32$ grids.

If the 1 is in any of the four "side" cells (any cell which is not the center or a corner), it can be seen that there is no such grid satisfying the requirements.

Therefore the number of possible grids is $8 + 32 = \boxed{40}$. □

Problem 24. In trapezoid $ABCD$, $\overline{AB} \parallel \overline{DC}$ and $m\angle DAB = 2m\angle ABC$. Given that $AD = DC = 1$ and $AB = 3$, what is BC?

A) 2   B) $\dfrac{5}{2}$ C) $\sqrt{3}$ D) $\sqrt{6}$ E) $\dfrac{7}{2}$

Solutions for Practice Exam 2

Solution. Draw $\overline{AC}$ and let $m\angle DCA = \alpha$.
As $AD = DC$ and $CD \parallel AB$, we have

$$m\angle DCA = m\angle DAC = m\angle CAB = \alpha.$$

As $m\angle DAB = 2m\angle ABC$, we also have $m\angle CBA = \alpha$. Therefore, $\triangle ADC \sim \triangle ACB$, and so

$$\frac{1}{x} = \frac{x}{3}$$

Hence, $x = \sqrt{3}$. The answer is $\boxed{C}$. □

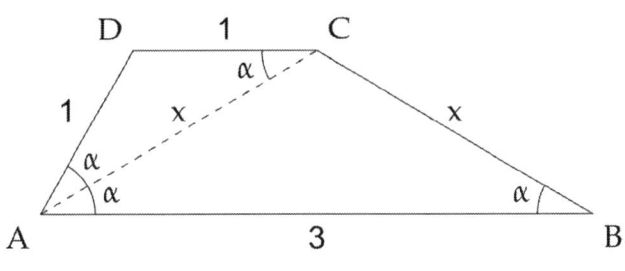

Problem 25. Suppose a and b are real numbers such that $ab^2 = 1$ and $a^3 + 3b^3 = 4$. What is the product of all possible values of $a^3 + b^3$?

A) 12 B) 18 C) 24 D) 36 E) 72

Solution. Cube both sides of the first equation to obtain $a^3b^6 = 1$, which may be written as $a^3(b^3)^2 = 1$. Note that a is necessarily positive, as $a = \frac{1}{b^2} > 0$. However b is not necessarily positive.
Hence we have a system of two equations in terms of a^3 and b^3. Let $a^3 = x$ and $b^3 = y$, where $x > 0$.

$$xy^2 = 1$$
$$x + 3y = 4$$

Substitute x with $4 - 3y$ into the first equation to obtain $(4 - 3y)y^2 = 1$, or $3y^3 - 4y^2 + 1 = 0$. Immediately we see that $y = 1$ is a solution; using long or synthetic division, we see the cubic equation factors as $(y - 1)(3y^2 - y - 1) = 0$. By the quadratic formula, the other two solutions are $y = \frac{1 \pm \sqrt{13}}{6}$.
If $y = 1$, then $x = 1$, which induces the solution $(a, b) = (1, 1)$. If $y = \frac{1+\sqrt{13}}{6}$, then using $x = 4 - 3y$ we obtain $x = \frac{7-\sqrt{13}}{2}$ which is positive. If $y = \frac{1-\sqrt{13}}{6}$, then $x = \frac{7+\sqrt{13}}{2}$. In all these cases, $(a, b) = (\sqrt[3]{x}, \sqrt[3]{y})$, and $a^3 + b^3$ is simply $x + y$.
The first solution gives $a^3 + b^3 = x + y = 2$. The second solution gives $x + y = \frac{11-\sqrt{13}}{3}$. The third solution gives $x + y = \frac{11+\sqrt{13}}{3}$. The product of all possible values of $a^3 + b^3$ (or $x + y$) is

$$2\left(\frac{11-\sqrt{13}}{3}\right)\left(\frac{11+\sqrt{13}}{3}\right) = \boxed{24}.$$

□

Solutions for Practice Exam 2

Problem 1. If $x + 4 = y^2 - 1 = z^2 + 2 = t - 3 = m^2 + 12$, which of the numbers x, y, z, t, and m is the greatest?

A) x B) y C) z D) t E) m

Solution. As $y^2 - 1 = z^2 + 2 = m^2 + 12$, the greatest value among y^2, z^2 and m^2 is y^2. On the other hand, as $x + 4 = t - 3$, the greatest value among x and t is t. Thus, when we compare t and y^2 by using $t - 3 = y^2 - 1$, we have $t = y^2 + 2$. That is, t is the greatest among all of them. The answer is $\boxed{D}$.

Problem 2. Suppose a and b are integers and $a + b$ is an odd number. Which of the following is always true?

     I) $a - 2b$ is even   II) $a \cdot b$ is even   III) $4a + b$ is even

A) Only I   B) Only II   C) Only III   D) I and II   E) I, II and III

Solution. Since $a + b$ is an odd number then a and b both cannot be odd or even at the same time. This lead us to decide $a \cdot b$ is always an even number since odd time even gives us always an even number. The other two options, I and III, don't always create an even number. The answer is $\boxed{B}$.

Problem 3. How many ways can the letters of the word TRIANGLE be arranged such that the letters ANGLE appear consecutively, and in that order?

A) 6   B) 18   C) 20   D) 24   E) 56

Solution. We consider ANGLE as a one piece. Then there are 4 pieces to arrange. Therefore there are $4! = 24$ ways. The answer is $\boxed{D}$.

Problem 4. What is the area of an isosceles triangle with side lengths 10, 10, and 12?

A) 48   B) 50   C) 60   D) 72   E) 96

Solution. Using Heron's area formula for triangles, the area of the triangle with sides 10, 10 and 12 is
$$\sqrt{16 \cdot (16 - 10) \cdot (16 - 10) \cdot (16 - 12)} = \sqrt{16 \cdot 6 \cdot 6 \cdot 4} = 48.$$
The answer is $\boxed{A}$.

Solutions for Practice Exam 2

Problem 5. In an online math practice test, Junaid attempts exactly $\frac{3}{4}$ of the problems and answers $\frac{5}{8}$ of those problems correctly. When he submits the test, he finds that he answered 105 problems correctly. How many math problems were on this test?

    A) 220   B) 224   C) 243   D) 248   E) None of the preceding

Solution. Letting N be the number of problems in the test, Junaid attemps $\frac{3N}{4}$ problems where $\frac{5}{8} \cdot \frac{3N}{4} = \frac{15N}{32}$ of them are correct. Since he answered 105 problems correctly, i.e. $105 = \frac{15N}{32}$, we have $N = 224$. The answer is $\boxed{B}$. $\square$

Problem 6. Distinct, nonzero digits A, B, and C are such that the three-digit numbers ABC, CAB, and BCA are divisible by 4, 5, and 9, respectively. What is the greatest possible value of $A \times B \times C$?

    A) 20   B) 180   C) 200   D) 210   E) 240

Solution. Since CAB is divisible by 5, the value of B is either 0 or 5. However, BCA is a three digit number, therefore $B = 5$. On the other hand, since ABC is divisible by 4, the value of BC is either 52 or 56. Finally, since BCA is divisible by 9, the value of A is either 2 or 7. Therefore, the greatest value of $A \cdot B \cdot C$ is $7 \cdot 5 \cdot 6 = 210$. The answer is $\boxed{D}$. $\square$

Problem 7. Set $A = \{-7, -6, -5, -4, -3, -2, -1, 1, 2, 3\}$. What is the probability that product of two randomly selected numbers is positive number?

    A) $\frac{1}{15}$ B) $\frac{4}{15}$ C) $\frac{7}{15}$ D) $\frac{8}{15}$ E) $\frac{14}{15}$

Solution. One can choose two random numbers from A in $C(10,2) = 45$ ways. Their product is positive when both of the numbers are positive or negative at the same time. That is, there are $C(7,2) + C(3,2) = 21 + 3 = 24$ such choices. Thus, the probability is $\frac{24}{45} = \frac{8}{15}$. The answer is $\boxed{D}$. $\square$

Problem 8. A rectangular box has integer side lengths in the ratio of $1 : \frac{3}{2} : 2$. Which of the following could be the volume of the box?

    A) 136   B) 148   C) 160   D) 192   E) 204

Solutions for Practice Exam 2

Solution. The lowest integer ratio corresponding to $1 : \frac{3}{2} : 2$ is $2 : 3 : 4$, i.e. the sides of the box are $2a, 3a$ and $4a$ for some integer a. Then the volume of the box is $24a^3$. Hence, it would be 192 for $a = 2$, while the others are not in the form $24a^3$. The answer is $\boxed{D}$. $\square$

Problem 9. If $A = \frac{21}{19} + \frac{11}{29}$, then which of the following equals $\frac{18}{29} - \frac{2}{19}$?

A) $2 - A$ B) $1 - A$ C) A D) $A + 1$ E) $A + 2$

Solution.
$$\frac{18}{29} - \frac{2}{19} = \left(1 - \frac{11}{29}\right) - \left(\frac{21}{19} - 1\right) = 2 - \left(\frac{11}{29} + \frac{21}{19}\right) = 2 - A.$$

The answer is $\boxed{A}$. $\square$

Problem 10. The first page number of a book is 1. The sum of page numbers in the book is less than 2020. If there were 1 more page, then the sum of page numbers in the book would be more than 2020. Find the number of pages of the book.

A) 59   B) 60   C) 61   D) 62   E) 63

Solution. Assume n is the last page of the book. Then we have

$$1 + \ldots + n = \frac{n \cdot (n+1)}{2} < 2020 \text{ and } 1 + \ldots + (n+1) = \frac{(n+1) \cdot (n+2)}{2} > 2020.$$

Since n is an integer, we have $n \leq 63$ in the first inequality, and $n + 1 \geq 64$ in the second inequality. Thus $n = 63$. The answer is $\boxed{E}$. $\square$

Problem 11. Alice and Bob each roll a fair 12-sided die. What is the probability that Alice's roll is greater than or equal to Bob's roll?

A) $\frac{11}{24}$ B) $\frac{1}{2}$ C) $\frac{25}{48}$ D) $\frac{13}{24}$ E) $\frac{7}{12}$

Solution. Let (a, b) be the tuple where the value of Alice's die is a and the value of Bob's die is b. There are $12 \cdot 12 = 144$ such tuples since $a, b \in \{1, 2, \ldots, 12\}$. The number of tuples where $a \geq b$ are

$$\#(a \geq 1) + \#(a \geq 2) + \ldots + \#(a \geq 12) = 12 + 11 + \ldots + 1 = 78.$$

Therefore, the probability that Alice's roll is greater than or equal to Bob's roll is $\frac{78}{144} = \frac{13}{24}$. The answer is $\boxed{D}$. $\square$

Solutions for Practice Exam 2

Problem 12. The diagram shows four identical rectangles placed inside a square. The perimeter of each rectangle is 24 cm. What is the perimeter of the large square?

A) 24 cm

B) 30 cm

C) 36 cm

D) 48 cm

E) 56 cm

Solution. Let x be the length of short edge of each identical rectangles. Then the length of long edge will be 12 − x since the perimeter is 24. Therefore, the length of each side of the square is x + (12 − x) = 12 and so the perimeter of the square is 48. The answer is $\boxed{D}$. □

Problem 13. The fraction $\frac{7}{13}$ is equal to $0.\overline{538461} = 0.5384615384615....$ What is the 2020th digit to the right of the decimal point?

A) 1 B) 3 C) 4 D) 5 E) 6

Solution. Each digit in $0.\overline{538461} = 0.5384615384615...$ is repeated after every 6 digits. Since $2020 \equiv 4 \mod 6$, the 2020th digit is 4. The answer is $\boxed{C}$. □

Problem 14. If $N = 2^3 \cdot 3^2 \cdot 7 \cdot n$, and N is divisible by 50, then which of the following *could* be the value of n?

A) 5 B) 15 C) 20 D) 40 E) 75

Solution. Since N is divisible by 50, n should be divisible by $5^2 = 25$. Therefore, the value of n could be 75. The answer is $\boxed{E}$. □

Problem 15. In a school of 300 students, there are 38 people on the football team and 30 people on the basketball team. If there are 252 students who play neither sport, how many students are on both teams?

A) 20 B) 24 C) 28 D) 32 E) None

Solution. There are 300 − 252 = 48 students either playing football or basketball. Then there are (38 + 30) − 48 = 20 students both playing football and basketball. The answer is $\boxed{A}$. □

Solutions for Practice Exam 2

Problem 16. The ratio of the corresponding side lengths of two similar triangles is 5 : 4, and the perimeter of the larger triangle is 30 cm. What is length the of the shortest side of the smaller triangle, if its side lengths are consecutive even numbers?

A) 10 cm B) 8 cm C) 6 cm D) 4 cm E) 2 cm

Solution. Since the similarity ratio is 5 : 4, the perimeter of the smaller triangle is $\frac{30 \cdot 4}{5} = 24$. Let the length of the shortest side of the smaller triangle be a. Then the other lengths are $a + 2$ and $a + 4$. Since $a + (a + 2) + (a + 4) = 24$, we have $a = 6$ as the solution of this equation. The answer is $\boxed{C}$. □

Problem 17. In the grid below, each of the 16 squares is to be filled with either 0 or 1 so that the sum of the four numbers in each row and column is even. In how many ways can this be done?

A) 2^9

B) 2^{10}

C) 2^{12}

D) 2^{15}

E) 2^{16}

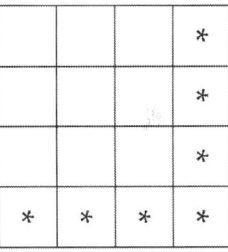

Solution. When we fill the top-left 3×3 square, then the remaining squares will be uniquely filled so that the sum is even. Hence, there are 2^9 ways. The answer is $\boxed{A}$. □

Problem 18. What is the number of ordered pairs (x, y) of positive integers that satisfy the equation?

$$2x + 3y = 120$$

A) 19 B) 24 C) 29 D) 36 E) None

Solution. We have $x = 60 - \frac{3y}{2}$. Since x is an integer, y should be divisible by 2, say $y = 2k$ for some positive integer k. Then $x = 60 - 3k$ and $y = 2k$. Then we have (x, y) solutions for $k = 1, 2, \ldots, 19$, that is, there are 19 solutions. The answer is $\boxed{A}$. □

Solutions for Practice Exam 2

Problem 19. If x, y, and z are three numbers picked randomly and with replacement from the set $\{1, 2, 3, 4, 5\}$ then what is the probability that $xz + y$ is even number?

A) $\dfrac{2}{5}$ B) $\dfrac{23}{25}$ C) $\dfrac{39}{125}$ D) $\dfrac{64}{125}$ E) $\dfrac{59}{125}$

Solution. The total number of outcomes is $5^3 = 125$. There are two cases:

1. Both xz and y are even. Then there are $(25 - 9) \cdot 2 = 32$ triples.

2. Both xz and y are odd. Then there are $9 \cdot 3 = 27$ triples.

So the probability that $xz + y$ is even number is $\dfrac{32 + 27}{125} = \dfrac{59}{125}$. The answer is $\boxed{E}$. □

Problem 20. Point P is on the same plane as $\triangle ABC$. For how many P are $\triangle PAB$, $\triangle PAC$, and $\triangle PBC$ isosceles?

A) 1   B) 6   C) 7   D) 10   E) 12

Solution. There is only one such P, which is the intersection of the perpendicular bisectors of $\overline{AB}$, $\overline{BC}$ and $\overline{AC}$. The answer is $\boxed{A}$. □

Problem 21. The real numbers a and b satisfy $a + b = 2$ and $a \cdot b = -1$. What is the value of

$$\frac{1}{a} + \frac{a^2}{b^3} + \frac{1}{b} + \frac{b^2}{a^3}?$$

A) −76   B) −80   C) −84   D) −88   E) None of the preceding

Solution. As $\dfrac{1}{a} = -b$ and $\dfrac{1}{b} = -a$, we have

$$\frac{1}{a} + \frac{a^2}{b^3} + \frac{1}{b} + \frac{b^2}{a^3} = -(a + b) - (a^5 + b^5).$$

We already know that $a + b = 2$. We need to compute $a^5 + b^5$. Notice that

$$(a + b)^5 = (a^5 + b^5) + 5ab(a^3 + b^3) + 10a^2b^2(a + b) \quad \text{and} \quad (a + b)^3 = (a^3 + b^3) + 3ab(a + b).$$

From the second equation, we have

$$a^3 + b^3 = 2^3 - 3(-1)(2) = 14,$$

and therefore,

$$a^5 + b^5 = 2^5 - 5(-1)(14) - 10(-1)^2(2) = 82.$$

Solutions for Practice Exam 2

Thus, the result is $-2 - 82 = -84$. The answer is $\boxed{C}$.

Alternative Solution.

$$\frac{1}{a} + \frac{a^2}{b^3} + \frac{1}{b} + \frac{b^2}{a^3} = \frac{a^2 b^3 + a^5 + b^2 a^3 + b^5}{a^3 b^3} = \frac{(a^2 + b^2)(a^3 + b^3)}{(ab)^3}.$$

We already have that $ab = -1$, we need to compute $a^2 + b^2$ and $a^3 + b^3$. However,

$$a^2 + b^2 = (a+b)^2 - 2ab = (2)^2 - 2(-1) = 6.$$

Morevoer,
$$a^3 + b^3 = (a+b)(a^2 + b^2 - ab) = (2)(6 - (-1)) = 14.$$

Thus, the answer is
$$\frac{(6)(14)}{(-1)^3} = -84.$$

□

Problem 22. What is the number of integer solutions (x, y) satisfying the equation

$$x \cdot y = 3x + 6y?$$

A) 0   B) 9   C) 12   D) 16   E) 18

Solution. $x \cdot y = 3x + 6y \implies x(y-3) = 6y = 6(y-3) + 18 \implies (x-6)(y-3) = 18$. Since each divisor of $18 = 2 \cdot 3^2$ gives an integer solution (x, y), there are $2 \times 2 \times 3 = 12$ solutions. The answer is $\boxed{C}$.

□

Problem 23. Gabby lives in a town whose streets are on a grid system with all streets running east-west or north-south without breaks. Her school, located on a corner, lies four blocks south and three blocks east of her home, also located on a corner. If Gabby only walks south or east on her way to school, how many possible routes can she take to school?

A) 20
B) 25
C) 30
D) 35
E) 40

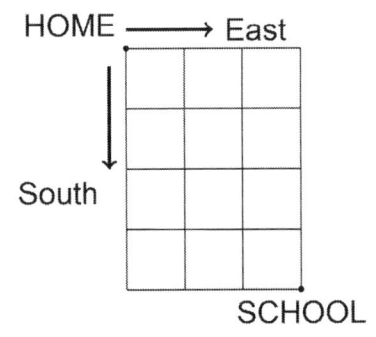

129

Solutions for Practice Exam 2

Solution. Give "values" to the each point on the grid as follows:"1" to the closest two points (since there is only one way to school), and, the sum of values of the point on the south and the point on the east. In the end, we have 35 ways to go to the school. The answer is $\boxed{D}$. □

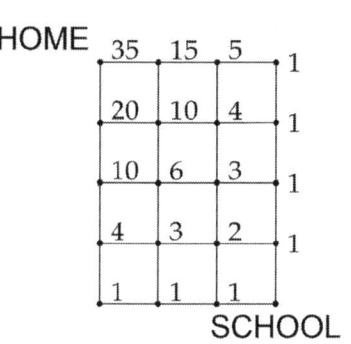

Problem 24. ABC is a right triangle with AB ⊥ AC and AD is angle bisector of ∠BAC. If $AD = 1$, what is the value of $\dfrac{1}{AB} + \dfrac{1}{AC}$?

A) $\sqrt{2}$ B) $\dfrac{3}{2}$ C) $\sqrt{2}+1$ D) $\dfrac{1+\sqrt{5}}{2}$ E) None of the preceding

Solution. Notice that the area of △ABC is the sum of the areas of △ABD and △ADC:

$$\frac{ab}{2} = \frac{a \cdot 1 \cdot \sin 45°}{2} + \frac{b \cdot 1 \cdot \sin 45°}{2}$$

This implies $ab = (a+b)\sin 45°$, that is,

$$\frac{1}{\sin 45°} = \frac{1}{a} + \frac{1}{b} = \frac{1}{AB} + \frac{1}{AC} = \sqrt{2}.$$

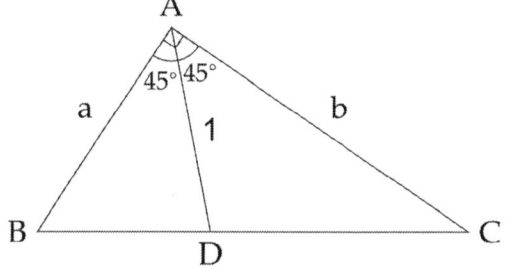

The answer is $\boxed{A}$. □

Problem 25. Three of 101 coins are fake. Weights of the fake coins are equivalent and lighter than the real coins. What is the minimum number of weightings to guarantee that we can find 25 real coins by using an equal arm balance?

A) 2 B) 3 C) 4 D) 5 E) None

Solution. We can start by partitioning 101 coins into 3 groups A, B and C of sizes 50, 50 and 1, respectively. Notice that either A or B includes at least two fake coins, because there are 3 fake coins in total. Comparing the weights of A and B, we have two cases:

1. If their weights are equal, each of A and B contains a fake coin (while C contains the other fake coin). Partition A into two subgroups A_1 and A_2 of sizes 25 and 25 and compare their weights. Their weights can not be equal, moreover, the group with heavy weight contains no fake coin. In total we use equal arm balance twice.

2. If the weights of A and B are not equal, we have another two sub-cases:

    (a) The heavier group contains no fake coins.
    (b) The heavier group contains one fake coin (and therefore the other contains two fake coins).

    For both sub-cases, partition the heavier group into two subgroups of sizes 25 and 25. If their weights are equal, it corresponds to the first sub-case, so we have 25 real coins in each subgroup. Otherwise, the heavier subgroup contains no fake coin, and therefore we again 25 real coins. In total we use the equal arm balance twice.

Thus, in both cases, we use the equal arm balance twice. The answer is $\boxed{A}$.

Solutions for Practice Exam 3

Problem 1. The sum of all integers from -13 to 14 (including -13 and 14) is A. The product of all these integers is B. Find $A + B$.

A) 0 B) 13 C) 14 D) 12584 E) None of the preceding

Solution. We have

$$A = (-13) + (-12) + \ldots + 14 = \underbrace{(-13 + 13)}_{0} + \underbrace{(-12 + 12)}_{0} + \ldots + \underbrace{(-1 + 1)}_{0} + 0 + 14 = 14$$

and
$$B = (-13) \times (-12) \times \ldots \times 0 \times \ldots 14 = 0$$

Hence, $A + B = 14$. The answer is $\boxed{C}$.

Problem 2. For how many positive values of n are both $\frac{n}{3}$ and $3n$ three digit integers?

A) 12 B) 15 C) 18 D) 21 E) 24

Solution. Notice that n is a multiple of 3, so $\frac{n}{3}$ is an integer. Also notice that

$$100 \leq \frac{n}{3} < 3n \leq 999,$$

in other words, $300 \leq n \leq 333$. Thus, there are 12 possible values for n: 300, 303, ..., 333. The answer is $\boxed{A}$.

Problem 3. The number 800 can be written as the product of two positive even integers. In how many ways can this be done?

A) 8 B) 7 C) 6 D) 5 E) 4

Solutions for Practice Exam 3

Solution. Notice that $800 = 2^5 \cdot 5^2 = (2 \cdot 2^a \cdot 5^b) \cdot (2 \cdot 2^{3-a} \cdot 5^{2-b})$. Then $a = 0, 1, 2, 3$ and $b = 0, 1, 2$. Also considering the symmetry, we have $\frac{4 \cdot 3}{2} = 6$ ways to write 800 as a product of two even numbers. The answer is $\boxed{C}$. □

Problem 4. What is the degree measure of the smaller angle formed by the hands of a clock at 8:15?

A) 150°   B) 157.5°   C) 165°   D) 172.5°   E) None of the preceding

Solution. At 8:00, the hour hand is on the 8 and the minute hand is on the 12, that is, the angle between the hands is 120°. Since the hour hand moves 30° and the minute hand moves 360° per hour, the hour hand moves 7.5° and the minute hand moves 90° after 15 minutes. Therefore, the angle between the hands is $120° + 90° - 7.5° = 202.5°$, or, $360° - 202.5° = 157.5°$. The answer is $\boxed{B}$. □

Problem 5. There are 19 figures consisting of triangles and squares. They have 68 edges in total. How many triangles are there?

A) 8   B) 9   C) 10   D) 11   E) 12

Solution. Suppose there are x triangles. Then, $68 = 3x + 4(19 - x)$, that is, $x = 8$. The answer is $\boxed{A}$. □

Problem 6. The five-digit number 3M8M5 is divisible by 9. What is the value of the digit M?

A) 0   B) 1   C) 2   D) 3   E) 4

Solution. A number is divisible by 9 if and only if the sum of its digits is divisible by 9. Therefore, $3 + M + 8 + M + 5 = 2M + 16$ is divisible by 9. This is only possible when $M = 1$. The answer is $\boxed{B}$. □

Problem 7. Three fair six-sided dice are rolled. What is the probability that the three dice all show the same number?

A) $\frac{1}{216}$ B) $\frac{1}{36}$ C) $\frac{1}{18}$ D) $\frac{1}{6}$ E) None of the preceding

Solution. There are $6^3 = 216$ triples (a, b, c) for three dice. The number of triples such that $a = b = c$ is 6. Thus, the probability is $\frac{6}{216} = \frac{1}{36}$. The answer is $\boxed{B}$. □

Solutions for Practice Exam 3

Problem 8. A cube is inscribed in a sphere. If the volume of the cube is 8, what is the surface area of the sphere?

A) $15\pi\sqrt{3}$ B) $12\pi\sqrt{2}$ C) 15π D) 12π E) None of the preceding

Solution. Notice that the side length of the cube is $a = 2$ because its volume is $a^3 = 8$. Then, since the diagonal of the cube is also the diameter of the sphere, we have $2r = a\sqrt{3} = 2\sqrt{3}$, i.e. $r = \sqrt{3}$. Thus, the surface area of the sphere is $4\pi r^2 = 12\pi$. The answer is $\boxed{D}$. □

Problem 9. A restaurant offers four desserts, and exactly twice as many appetizers as main courses. A dinner consists of an appetizer, a main course, and a dessert. What is the least number of main courses that the restaurant should offer so that a customer could have a different dinner each night for a year?

A) 5 B) 6 C) 7 D) 8 E) 9

Solution. Suppose there are A main courses. Then, there are 2A types of appetizers. A customer could have a different dinner each night for a year if

$$4 \times 2A \times A \geq 365.$$

That is, $A^2 \geq \frac{365}{8}$. The least possible value for A is 7. The answer is $\boxed{C}$. □

Problem 10. The number 100 has nine factors: 1, 2, 4, 5, 10, 20, 25, 50, and 100. How many factors does 900 have?

A) 11 B) 18 C) 27 D) 45 E) 81

Solution. Notice that $900 = 9 \cdot 100$. Then a factor of 900 can be expressed as $a \cdot b$ such that a is a divisor of 9 and b is a divisor of 100. We already know that there are 9 candidates for b. On the other hand, 9 has 3 factors: 1, 3 and 9, so there are 3 candidates for a. Hence, we have $3 \cdot 9 = 27$ candidates for $a \cdot b$. The answer is $\boxed{C}$. □

Problem 11. Five companies each send three representatives to a networking event. At the event, each representative must shake hands with all the representatives from companies other than their own. How many handshakes must take place?

A) 72 B) 90 C) 108 D) 120 E) 156

Solution. There are 15 representatives in total. So there are $C(15, 2)$ handshakes without any restriction. However we want each representative to shake hands with all the representatives from companies other than their own, so we need to exclude $C(3, 2)$ handshakes per company. Thus our answer is $C(15, 2) - 5 \cdot C(3, 2) = 90$. The answer is $\boxed{B}$. □

Solutions for Practice Exam 3

Problem 12. Suppose $\overline{BD}$ bisects $\angle ABC$, $\overline{AC} \cap \overline{BD} = \{E\}$, $m\angle ACB = 50°$, and $m\angle ACD = 65°$. What is the value of $m\angle ADB$?

A) 20°
B) 25°
C) 30°
D) 35°
E) None of the preceding

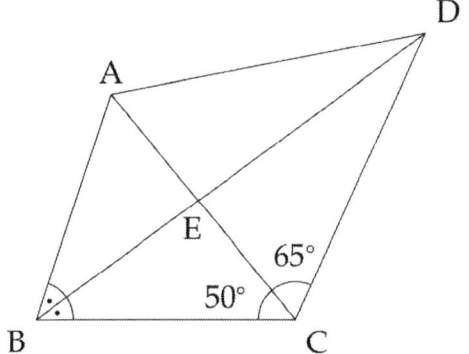

Solution. Extend $\overline{BC}$ to a line and pick a point F on the right of C.

Notice that $m\angle ACD = m\angle DCF = 65°$, that is, $\overline{DC}$ is the external bisector of $\angle ACF$. Since $\overline{BD}$ is also a bisector, $\overline{AD}$ is an outer bisector and D is the center of an outer tangent circle of ABC. Then

$$m\angle ADB = \frac{m\angle ACB}{2} = 25°.$$

The answer is $\boxed{B}$.

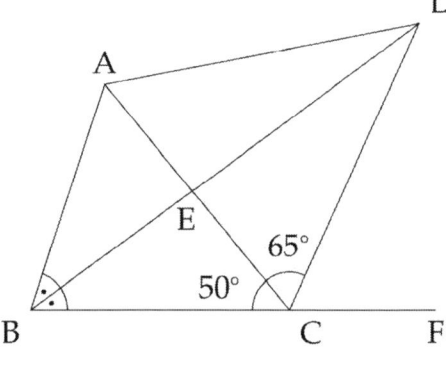

Problem 13. How many minutes between 3:59 p.m. and 4:59 p.m. on the same day will all three digits in a digital clock display be even?

A) 10   B) 12   C) 14   D) 15   E) 16

Solution. The time on the digital clock should be in the form 4 : ab where a and b are even digits. Since there are three digits for a (i.e. 0, 2, 4) and five digits for b (i.e. 0, 2, 4, 6, 8), there are 15 possible values for ab. The answer is $\boxed{D}$.

Problem 14. How many digits are there in the number $125^4 \cdot 64^2$, when expressed as a base-10 integer?

A) 10   B) 11   C) 12   D) 13   E) 14

Solution. $125^4 \cdot 64^2 = (5^3)^4 \cdot (2^6)^2 = 5^{12} \cdot 2^{12} = 10^{12} = 1\underbrace{0...0}_{12}$ has 13 digits. The answer is $\boxed{D}$.

Solutions for Practice Exam 3

Problem 15. A *palindrome* is a positive whole number which reads the same forwards and backwards. For example, 7, 11, and 252 are all palindromes. How many *palindromes* are less than 1,000?

    A) 81   B) 90   C) 99   D) 108   E) 126

Solution. Notice that each one-digit number is a palindrome. On the other hand, a two-digit number ab is a palindrome if and only if $a = b$. Lastly, a three-digit number abc is a palindrome if and only if $a = c$. Thus, there are $9 + 9 + 9 \cdot 10 = 108$ palindromes less than 1000. The answer is $\boxed{D}$. □

Problem 16. Equilateral $\triangle ADE$ shares a side with square ADCF. What is the sum of $m\angle FEC$ and $m\angle DEC$?

A) 195°

B) 200°

C) 215°

D) 225°

E) 245°

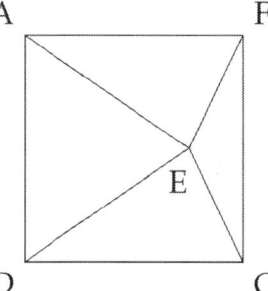

Solution. Since $\triangle ADE$ is equilateral and ADCF is a square, we have $AF = AE$ and $DE = DC$. Then $\triangle AFE$ and $\triangle DCE$ are $30° - 75° - 75°$ triangles. So $m\angle FEC = 360° - (60° + 75° + 75°) = 150°$. Thus

$$m\angle FEC + m\angle DEC = 150° + 75° = 225°.$$

The answer is $\boxed{D}$. □

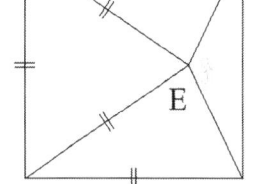

Problem 17. If a and b are positive integers with $(b-1)^{a+b} = 2^6$, then the number of possible values for a is

    A) 1   B) 2   C) 3   D) 4   E) 6

Solution. The candidates for $b - 1$ are 2, 4, 8, or 64, so b is either 3, 5, 9, or 65. Only $b = 3$ gives a solution for a. The answer is $\boxed{A}$. □

Problem 18. $T(n)$ is the sum of the digits of the positive integer n. (e.g. $T(5081) = 5+0+8+1 = 14$) Find the number n that satisfies $T(n) + 3n = 2020$.

A) 666 B) 667 C) 668 D) 669 E) None of the preceding

Solution. Notice that $1 \leq T(n) \leq 27$ for any three-digit number n. Since $T(n) = 2020 - 3n$, we have
$$1 \leq 2020 - 3n \leq 27,$$
in other words, $665 \leq n \leq 673$. It can be checked that the only number n in this interval satisfying the equation $T(n) + 3n = 2020$ is $n = 667$. The answer is $\boxed{B}$. □

Problem 19. In a regular decagon, all diagonals are drawn. If a diagonal is chosen at random, what is the probability it is neither one of the shortest nor one of the longest?

A) $\dfrac{2}{7}$ B) $\dfrac{3}{7}$ C) $\dfrac{12}{35}$ D) $\dfrac{4}{9}$ E) $\dfrac{4}{7}$

Solution. There are $\dfrac{10 \cdot 7}{2} = 35$ diagonals in total. Label the vertices as $0, 1, \ldots, 9$, and denote the diagonal joining the vertices a and b by ab. There are 10 shortest diagonals, which are 02, 08, 13, 19, 24, 35, 46, 57, 68, 79. On the other hand, there are 5 longest diagonals, which are 05, 16, 27, 38, 49. Thus, the probability that the chosen diagonal is neither one of the shortest nor one of the longest is
$$1 - \dfrac{10+5}{35} = \dfrac{4}{7}$$

The answer is $\boxed{E}$. □

Problem 20. ABCD is a convex pentagon with $m\angle B = m\angle D = 90°$ and $m\angle C = 120°$. Given that $AB = 4$, $BC = CD = 2\sqrt{3}$, and $ED = 2$, what is AE?

A) $\sqrt{3}$ B) $\dfrac{3}{2}$ C) $\dfrac{3\sqrt{3}}{2}$ D) $2\sqrt{3}$ E) None of the preceding

Solution. Join the points E and C. Since
$$CD = ED \cdot \sqrt{3}$$
in the right triangle EDC, we have $m\angle DEC = 60°$ and $m\angle ECD = 30°$ and $EC = 4$. Then,
$$m\angle ECB = 120° - 30° = 90°.$$

Then, AEBC is a rectangle. because $AB = EC = 4$ and $m\angle B = m\angle BCE = 90°$. Thus, $AE = 2\sqrt{3}$. The answer is $\boxed{D}$. □

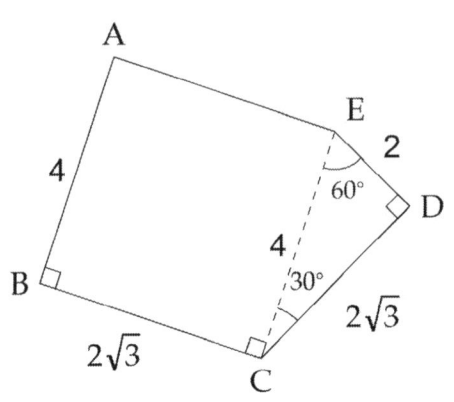

Solutions for Practice Exam 3

Problem 21. x is a real number satisfying $(x - 3)^{x^2-9} = 1$. What is the sum of all possible values of x?

A) 1 B) 3 C) 4 D) 7 E) 8

Solution. There are three cases: either $x - 3 = 1$, or $(x - 3) = -1$ but $x^2 - 9$ is even, or $x^2 - 9 = 0$ but $x - 3 \neq 0$. In the first case, we have $x = 4$. In the second case, there is no solution. In the third case, $x = -3$. Thus, the sum of all possible values of x is $4 + (-3) = 1$. The answer is $\boxed{A}$. □

Problem 22. If a, b and c are distinct prime numbers with $a - c = 5094$ and $a + b + c = 5242$, then what is the value of $a + 2b$?

A) 5167 B) 5171 C) 5176 D) 6002 E) None of the preceding

Solution. As $a + b + c$ is even, one of a, b, c is an even prime, that is, 2. As $a - c$ is even, both a and c are odd. So $b = 2$. From the equations $a - c = 5094$ and $a + c = 5240$, we have $a = 5167$ and $c = 73$. So $a + 2b = 5171$. The answer is $\boxed{B}$. □

Problem 23. 5 soccer teams participate in a tournament. Each team plays all the other teams exactly once. If a team wins a game, 3 points are awarded. If a team loses a game, no points are awarded. If the game is tie, both teams get 1 point. At the end of all the games, 4 of the 5 teams get 1, 2, 5, and 8 points in total. What is the total score of the fifth team?

A) 10 B) 12 C) 14 D) 16 E) None

Solution. Let W, L and T represent a win, a lose and a tie respectively. Let A, B, C and D be the four teams who gets 1, 2, 5 and 8 points in total, respectively. Let E be the fifth team.

Neither A nor B has a win, since both of them have fewer than 3 points, i.e. no wins. So A has $\{T, L, L, L\}$ and B has $\{T, T, L, L\}$. Moreover, the match between A and B must be a tie. Thus A lost its matches against C, D, E.

Since C has a win against A and 5 points in total, C has $\{W, T, T, L\}$. Then the match between B and C must be a tie, since neither B or C has any other wins. Thus B lost its matches against D and E.

Since D has two wins against A and B, and 8 points in total, D has $\{W, W, T, T\}$, i.e. its matches against C or E are ties.

Finally, E has a win against A, B and C, while it has a tie against D. So its total number of points is $3 \cdot 2 + 1 = 10$. The answer is $\boxed{A}$. □

137

Solutions for Practice Exam 4

Problem 24. ABC is a triangle with integer side lengths and AC = 56. Point D is on BC such that AD is angle bisector of ∠BAC. Given that AB = DC, what is BC?

A) 42
B) 48
C) 66
D) 70
E) 72

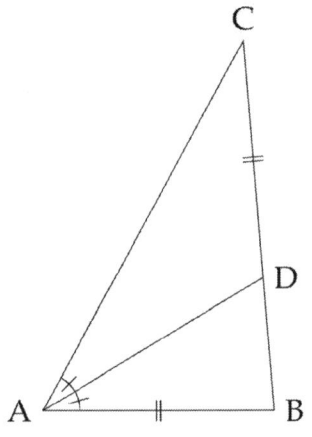

Solution. Let $AB = DC = x$ and $BD = y$. Since $\overline{AD}$ is bisector of m∠BAD, we have $\dfrac{56}{x} = \dfrac{x}{y}$, that is,

$$x^2 = 56y = 4 \cdot 14 \cdot y.$$

Since the side lengths have integer values, we have $y = 14k^2$ and $x = 28k$ for some positive integer k. Using the triangle inequality, $y < 56 < 2x + y$, that is,

$$14k^2 < 56 < 56k + 14k^2.$$

The only positive integer value satisfying the inequality is $k = 1$. Then $x = 28$ and $y = 14$, therefore, $BC = x + y = 42$. The answer is $\boxed{A}$. □

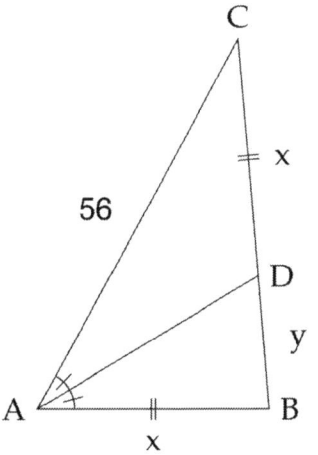

Problem 25. How many pairs (x, y) of positive integers are there so that $3x + 5y = 613$?

A) 23 B) 29 C) 35 D) 41 E) 45

Solution. Since $3x + 5y = 613 \implies 3x \equiv 3 \mod 5 \implies x \equiv 1 \mod 5$, we have $x = 5k + 1$ for some integer k. Then $y = 122 - 3k$. Thus, $0 \leq k \leq 40$, that is, there are 41 pairs (x, y). The answer is $\boxed{D}$. □

Solutions for Practice Exam 4

Problem 1. Which of the following is equal to $\dfrac{3^8 + 3^8 + 3^8}{9^4 + 9^4 + 9^4}$?

Solutions for Practice Exam 4

A) $\dfrac{1}{2}$ B) $\dfrac{1}{3}$ C) 1   D) 3   E) None of the preceding

Solution.
$$\frac{3^8+3^8+3^8}{9^4+9^4+9^4} = \frac{3\cdot 3^8}{3\cdot 9^4} = \frac{3^9}{3\cdot 3^8} = \frac{3^9}{3^9} = 1.$$

The answer is $\boxed{C}$.

Problem 2. The sequence 1, 8, 27, 64, ..., ends with 1,000,000. How many terms are in the sequence?

A) 99   B) 100   C) 999   D) 1000   E) 10001

Solution. The numbers in the sequence are perfect cubes, i.e. $1^3, 2^3, 3^3, 4^3, ..., 100^3$. Therefore, there are 100 terms in the sequence. The answer is $\boxed{B}$.

Problem 3. In a class, 10 students use social media A, 9 students use social media B, 6 students use both social media A and social media B, and 2 students use neither social media A nor social media B. What is the probability of selecting a student from this class at random who uses only social media B?

A) $\dfrac{1}{5}$ B) $\dfrac{4}{15}$ C) $\dfrac{2}{5}$ D) $\dfrac{3}{5}$ E) $\dfrac{1}{15}$

Solution. The number of students who use social media is $10+9-6=13$. Thus, there are $13+2=15$ students in the class. On the other hand, there are $9-6=3$ students who use only social media B. Then, the probability of selecting a student from this class at random who uses only social media B is $\dfrac{3}{15}=\dfrac{1}{5}$. The answer is $\boxed{A}$.

Problem 4. At 6:30, what is the acute angle formed by the minute hand and hour hand of a 12-hour clock?

A) 10°   B) 15°   C) 20°   D) 25°   E) 30°

Solution. At 6:00, the hour hand is on the 6 and the minute hand is on the 12, that is, the angle between the hands is 180°. Since the hour hand moves 15° and the minute hand moves 180° after 30 minutes. The angle between the hands is $180° + 15° - 180° = 15°$. The answer is $\boxed{B}$.

Solutions for Practice Exam 4

Problem 5. x, y and z are three numbers such that $x - y = y + z = 3$ and $y \neq 0$. What is the value of $\dfrac{x^2 - z^2}{y}$?

A) 4 B) 6 C) 10 D) 12 E) The answer depends on y.

Solution. By using the given equation, we have $x = 3 + y$ and $z = 3 - y$. That is, $x - z = 2y$ and $x + z = 6$. Thus,
$$\frac{x^2 - z^2}{y} = \frac{(x-z)(x+z)}{y} = \frac{12y}{y} = 12.$$
The answer is $\boxed{D}$.

Problem 6. For how many whole numbers x is $\dfrac{12}{x+2}$ an integer?

A) 12 B) 10 C) 8 D) 6 E) 5

Solution. The given fraction is an integer when $x + 2$ divides 12. That is, $x + 2$ is one of the divisors of 12: $\pm 1, \pm 2, \pm 3, \pm 4, \pm 6, \pm 12$. However, since x is a whole number, the possible values for x are $0, 1, 2, 4, 10$. The answer is $\boxed{E}$.

Problem 7. Students at Taylor Swift Middle School are assigned identification numbers with a capital letter followed by three digits, such as E482 or Q635. How many different identification numbers are possible?

A) 10,000 B) 20,000 C) 24,000 D) 26,000 E) 36,000

Solution. There are 26 candidates for the capital letter, and $10^3 = 1000$ candidates for the three digits. Hence, there are 26000 different identification numbers. The answer is $\boxed{D}$.

Problem 8. The vertices of a triangle are (1,1), (5,4), and (3,4). What is the area of the triangle?

A) 3 B) $\dfrac{7}{2}$ C) 4 D) $\dfrac{9}{2}$ E) 5

Solution. From the figure, we have $AH = 3$ and $BC = 2$. Thus, the area of ABC is $\dfrac{3 \cdot 2}{2} = 3$. The answer is $\boxed{A}$.

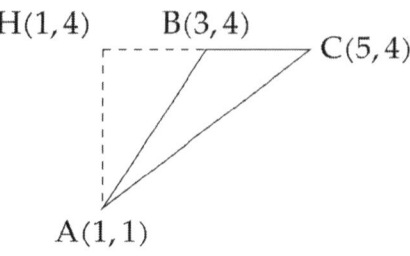

Solutions for Practice Exam 4

Problem 9. Suppose x and y are integers with $3^{2x} - 4^y = 77$. What is the value of $x + y$?

A) 2   B) 3   C) 4   D) 5   E) 7

Solution. $77 = 3^{2x} - 4^y = (3^x)^2 - (2^y)^2 = (3^x - 2^y)(3^x + 2^y)$. As x and y are integers, we have two cases: 1) $3^x - 2^y = 1$ and $3^x + 2^y = 77$, or 2) $3^x - 2^y = 7$ and $3^x + 2^y = 11$. There is no solution in the first case, but we have $3^x = 9$ and $2^y = 2$ in the second case. Thus, $x = 2$ and $y = 1$. The answer is $\boxed{B}$. □

Problem 10. For how many integers n is $|n^2 - 6n + 5|$ prime?

A) 1   B) 2   C) 3   D) 4   E) 5

Solution. Notice that $|n^2 - 6n + 5| = |(n-1)(n-5)| = |n-1| \cdot |n-5|$. Then, $|n^2 - 6n + 5|$ is prime when only one of $|n-1|$ and $|n-5|$ is 1. This is possible when n is either 0, 2, 4 or 6. It can be verified that $|n^2 - 6n + 5|$ is prime for all possible values of n. The answer is $\boxed{D}$. □

Problem 11. Start with 243. In each blank below, insert either ×3 or ÷9 to create a true equation. How many different true equations can be formed?

243 ___ ___ ___ ___ ___ ___ ___ = 1

A) 5   B) 12   C) 35   D) 128   E) 256

Solution. As all of $243 = 3^5$, $3 = 3^1$, $9 = 3^2$ and $1 = 3^0$ are powers of 3, we focus on their exponents. Notice that the exponent is increased by 1 when we insert ×3, and the exponent is decreased by 2 when we insert ÷9. Since there are 7 blanks in total, we should use ×3 three times and ÷9 four times. Also notice that it does not matter in which order we arrange them. Therefore, it is enough to choose three blanks to insert ×3. Thus, there are $C(7,3) = 35$ ways to form the equation. The answer is $\boxed{C}$. □

Problem 12. Given that ABCDEFGH is a regular octagon, what is m∠AGH?

A) 15°   B) 22.5°   C) 25°   D) 27.5°   E) 30°

Solutions for Practice Exam 4

Solution. Notice that measure of the interior angle in a regular octagon is $180° - \frac{360°}{8} = 135°$. Besides, HAG is an isosceles triangle. Therefore

$$m\angle AGH = \frac{180° - 135°}{2} = 22.5°.$$

The answer is $\boxed{B}$.

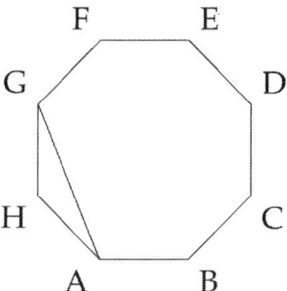

Problem 13. The first page number of a book is 1. The sum of page numbers of the book is less than 4040. If there were 1 more page, then the sum of page numbers of the book would be more than 4040. Find the number of pages of the book.

A) 89 B) 90 C) 91 D) 90 E) 93

Solution. Assume n is the last page of the book. Then we have

$$1 + \ldots + n = \frac{n \cdot (n+1)}{2} < 4040 \text{ and } 1 + \ldots + (n+1) = \frac{(n+1) \cdot (n+2)}{2} > 4040.$$

Since n is an integer, we have $n \leq 89$ in the first inequality, and $n + 1 \geq 90$ in the second inequality. Thus $n = 89$. The answer is $\boxed{A}$.

Problem 14. Suppose x and y are integers such that $x(y+1) = 8$ and $y(x+1) = 9$. What is the smallest value of $x + y$?

A) −7 B) −4 C) −3 D) 4 E) None of the preceding

Solution. From the given equations, we have $xy = 8 - x = 9 - y$. Therefore, $y = x + 1$. Using the second equation, we have $9 = y(x+1) = y^2$, i.e. $y = \pm 3$. Then $x = 2$ or $x = -4$, and therefore the smallest value of $x + y$ is $(-4) + (-3) = -7$. The answer is $\boxed{A}$.

Problem 15. A point X is selected uniformly at random inside square ABCD with side length 6. What is the probability that the area that the area of the quadrilateral ABXD is greater than 18?

A) $\frac{1}{6}$ B) $\frac{1}{4}$ C) $\frac{1}{3}$ D) $\frac{1}{2}$ E) $\frac{6}{19}$

Solution. The area of the square is 36 and the half of the area is 18. So, if we replace point X on the diagonal the square then the area of the quadrilateral ABXD (in this case it turns a triangle) become 18. However, if you replace point X in anywhere in the triangle BCD then we get an area that greater than 18. The answer is $\boxed{D}$.

Solutions for Practice Exam 4

Problem 16. Let ABC be acute triangle. If the angles of ABC, in degrees, are integers and form an arithmetic sequence. How many different possible triangles can be formed?

A) 30 B) 31 C) 33 D) 34 E) 36

Solution. We can make a list of all possible triples starting with (31,60,89) until (60,60,60). The answer is $\boxed{A}$.

Problem 17. What is the sum of all real values x which satisfy the following equation?

$$\left(\frac{x}{2} - 3\right)^{x+2} = 1$$

A) 6 B) 7 C) 8 D) 10 E) 12

Solution. There are three cases: i) $\frac{x}{2} - 3 = 1$, or ii) $\frac{x}{2} - 3 = -1$ and $x+2$ is even, iii) $x+2 = 0$ but $\frac{x}{2} - 3 \neq 0$. Hence, x is either 8 or 4 or -2. Hence the result is $8 + 4 + (-2) = 10$. The answer is $\boxed{D}$.

Problem 18. How many ordered integer pairs (x, y) satisfy the following equation?

$$(y + x)(y - x) = 111 + 6y$$

A) 2 B) 4 C) 8 D) 12 E) 16

Solution.
$$y^2 - x^2 = (y+x)(y-x) = 111 + 6y \Rightarrow y^2 - x^2 - 6y + 9 = 120$$
$$\Rightarrow (y-3)^2 - x^2 = 120 \Rightarrow (y - 3 + x)(y - 3 - x) = 120$$

Since 120 and $(y - 3 + x) - (y - 3 - x) = 2x$ are even, both $(y - 3 + x)$ and $(y - 3 - x)$ should be even. Say $y - 3 - x = 2k$, then $y - 3 + x = 2k + 2x$. Simplifying,

$$k(k + x) = 30$$

We can find a solution (x, y) for each divisor k of 30. Thus, the number of pairs is 16. The answer is $\boxed{E}$.

Problem 19. Two different whole numbers are randomly selected from the set $\{1, 2, 3, \ldots, 10\}$. What is the probability that their product is an even number?

A) $\frac{2}{9}$ B) $\frac{5}{9}$ C) $\frac{2}{3}$ D) $\frac{3}{4}$ E) $\frac{7}{9}$

Solutions for Practice Exam 4

Solution. Suppose x and y are two different numbers randomly chosen from the set $\{1, 2, 3, \ldots, 10\}$. Notice that there are $C(10, 2) = 45$ ways to choose such two numbers. Since

$$\Pr[x \cdot y \text{ is even}] = 1 - \Pr[x \cdot y \text{ is odd}],$$

and $x \cdot y$ is odd when both x and y are odd, we have

$$\Pr[x \cdot y \text{ is odd}] = \frac{C(5, 2)}{45} = \frac{10}{45} = \frac{2}{9}.$$

Thus, $\Pr[x \cdot y \text{ is even}] = \frac{7}{9}$. The answer is $\boxed{E}$. □

Problem 20. ABCD is a parallelogram. $CE = 3 \cdot ED$, $BF = FC$ and $KF = 6$. Find AK.

A) 10
B) 12
C) 14
D) 15
E) 16

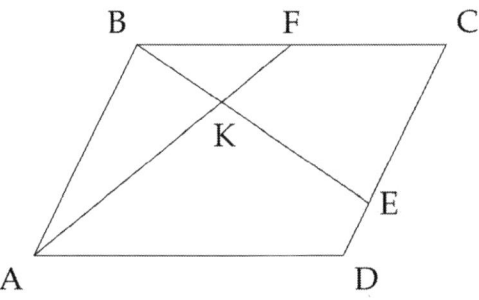

Solution. Let $ED = x$ and $AK = y$. Then $CE = 3x$ and $AB = 4x$. Since $BF = FC$, we have $GC = 4x$ and $GF = y + 6$ by similarity on $\triangle ABF$ and $\triangle GCF$. We have another similarity on $\triangle ABK$ and $\triangle GEK$, so $\frac{4x}{7x} = \frac{y}{y + 12}$. Solving this equation, we have $y = 16$. The answer is $\boxed{E}$. □

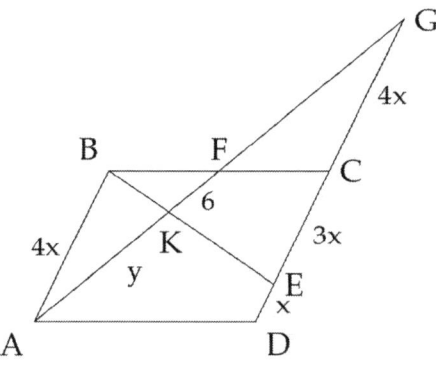

Problem 21. If $a^2 = 2020$, then what is the exact value of $\dfrac{a^3 - 3a^2 - a + 3}{a - 3}$?

A) 2018 B) 2019 C) 2020^2 D) $2020^3 - 2020^2$ E) None of the preceding

Solution.

$$\frac{a^3 - 3a^2 - a + 3}{a - 3} = \frac{(a - 3)(a^2 - 1)}{a - 3} = a^2 - 1 = 2020 - 1 = 2019.$$

The answer is $\boxed{B}$. □

144

Solutions for Practice Exam 4

Problem 22. What is the sum of all positive integers $n \neq 3$ such that the quantity $\dfrac{n^3 - 3}{n - 3}$ is an integer?

 A) 27 B) 34 C) 60 D) 84 E) 87

Solution. Notice that
$$\frac{n^3 - 3}{n - 3} = (n^2 + 3n + 9) + \frac{24}{n - 3}.$$

Then $\dfrac{n^3 - 3}{n - 3}$ is an integer only if $n - 3$ divides 24. Considering all divisors of 24, i.e. $\pm 1, \pm 2, \pm 3, \pm 4, \pm 6, \pm 8, \pm 12$ and ± 24, the candidates for n are 1, 2, 4, 5, 6, 7, 9, 11, 15 and 27. The answer is $\boxed{E}$. □

Problem 23. How many ordered triples (a, b, c) of positive integers are solutions to the inequality $a + b + c \leq 20$?

 A) 171 B) 231 C) 1140 D) 1771 E) None of the preceding

Solution. Let's use a dummy variable d such that $d = 20 - a - b - c$. Then we will count the number of solutions to $a + b + c + d = 20$ with $a, b, c \geq 1$. This is equivalent to counting the number of non-negative solutions to $a' + b' + c' + d = 17$. Then the result is $C(17 + 4 - 1, 4 - 1) = C(20, 3) = 1140$. The answer is $\boxed{C}$. □

Problem 24. For a triangle ABC, suppose the bisector of $\angle ABC$ intersects AC at the point D. If $BD = 3\sqrt{5}$, $AB = 8$, and $CD = \dfrac{3}{2}$, what is $AD + BC$?

A) 4
B) 6
C) 8
D) 10
E) None of the preceding

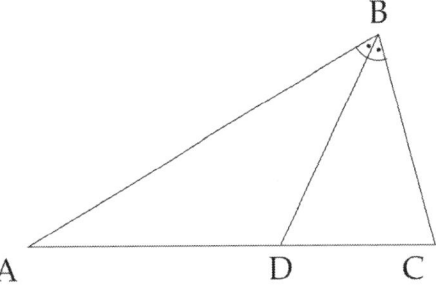

Solution. Let $AD = x$ and $BC = y$. Using the bisector formula, we have
$$\frac{AB}{AD} = \frac{BC}{CD} \quad \text{and} \quad BD^2 = AB \cdot BC - AD \cdot CD.$$

That is,
$$\frac{8}{x} = \frac{y}{3/2} \quad \text{and} \quad (3\sqrt{5})^2 = 45 = 8y - 3x/2.$$

Solutions for Practice Exam 5

From the first equation, we have $xy = 12$. When we multiply the second equation by x, we have
$$45x = 8xy - 3x^2/2 = 96 - 3x^2/2.$$
That is, x is a root of the quadratic equation $x^2 + 30x - 64 = 0$. Then, $x = 2$, and therefore, $y = 6$. Thus, $AD + BC = 8$. The answer is $\boxed{C}$. □

Problem 25. Suppose p_1, p_2, and p_3 are prime numbers that satisfy $p_1 + p_2 = (p_1 - p_2 + p_3) \cdot p_3$ and $p_1 + p_2 \leq 60$. What is the maximum value of $p_1 \cdot p_2 \cdot p_3$?

A) Between 201 and 300   B) Between 601 and 700   C) Between 701 and 800   D) Between 801 and 900   E) None of the preceding

Solution. Since we want to maximize the product $p_1 \cdot p_2 \cdot p_3$, suppose both p_1 and p_2 are odd. Then, both $p_1 + p_2$ and $p_1 - p_2$ are even. Then p_3 must be even, that is, $p_3 = 2$. Hence, using the given equation, we have
$$p_1 + p_2 = (p_1 - p_2 + 2) \cdot 2 \implies p_2 = \frac{p_1 + 4}{3}.$$
Since $p_1 + p_2 \leq 60$, the maximum value of p_1 and p_2 are 29 and 11 respectively. Thus, the product is $29 \cdot 11 \cdot 2 = 638$. The answer is $\boxed{B}$. □

Solutions for Practice Exam 5

Problem 1. Ashley and Kim want to begin a jogging routine. The local park's trail is only 30% of Ashley's distance goal and 50% of Kim's, so instead of jogging together, they decide to each jog from their homes to the library, play a game of chess, and each jog back home, which will exactly meet each runner's goal. If Ashley lives 1.8 miles from the library, how far from the library does Kim live?

A) 0.54 miles   B) 0.6 miles   C) 1.08 miles   D) 1.1 miles   E) 1.2 miles

Solution. Let $100x$ be Ashley's distance goal. Then, the length of the local park's trail is $0.30 \cdot 100x = 30x$. Then, Kim's goal is $30x/0.50 = 60x$. As Ashley lives 1.8 miles from the library, we have $100x = 2 \cdot 1.8$ miles $= 3.6$ miles. That is, $x = 0.036$ miles. Then Kim lives $60x/2 = 30x = 1.08$ miles from the library. The answer is $\boxed{C}$. □

Problem 2. Suppose x and y are positive integers such that $26 \cdot 27 \cdot 28 \cdot \ldots \cdot 100 = 5^x \cdot y$. What is the largest possible value of x?

A) 15   B) 16   C) 17   D) 18   E) 19

Solution. There are 15 numbers $(30, 35, \ldots, 100)$ between 26 and 100 which are divisible by 5. Three of them $(50, 75$ and $100)$ are divisible by 5^2. Therefore, the largest possible value of x is $15 + 3 = 18$. The answer is $\boxed{D}$. □

Solutions for Practice Exam 5

Problem 3. All two digit numbers are written on different cards and put in a drawing box. When you draw one card, what is the probability that at most two of the digits are 3?

A) $\dfrac{1}{9}$ B) $\dfrac{1}{5}$ C) $\dfrac{1}{30}$ D) $\dfrac{1}{15}$ E) 1

Solution. The case "at most two of the digits are 3" involves all two-digit numbers. Thus, the probability is 1. The answer is $\boxed{E}$. □

Problem 4. Given a triangle ABC, the angle bisector of $\angle BAC$ intersects $\overline{BC}$ at the point D. If $m\angle ADB = 80°$ and $m\angle B = 2m\angle C$, what is the value of $m\angle B$?

A) 20°
B) 25°
C) 30°
D) 35°
E) 40°

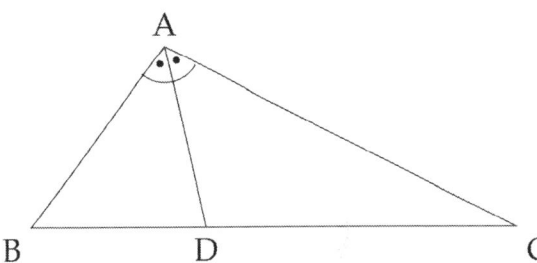

Solution. Let $m\angle BAD = m\angle DAC = x$. Then $m\angle C = 80° - x$. Since $m\angle B = 2m\angle C$, we have $m\angle B = 160° - 2x$. Then, because the sum of the internal angles on a triangle is 180°, we have
$$180° = m\angle A + m\angle B + m\angle C = 2x + 160° - 2x + 80° - x = 240° - x.$$
That is, $x = 60°$ and therefore $m\angle B = 40°$. The answer is $\boxed{E}$. □

Problem 5. Suppose a and b are non-zero additive inverses (opposites) of each other. What is the value of the following expression?

$$2(a+b-1)^{2019} + 3\left(\dfrac{a}{b}\right)^{2020} + 2019$$

A) 1 B) 2017 C) 2019 D) 2020 E) None of the preceding

Solution. Since a and b are non-zero additive inverses, we have $a = -b$. Then
$$2(a+b-1)^{2019} + 3\left(\dfrac{a}{b}\right)^{2020} + 2019 = 2(-1)^{2019} + 3(-1)^{2020} + 2019 = -2 + 3 + 2019 = 2020.$$

The answer is $\boxed{D}$. □

Solutions for Practice Exam 5

Problem 6. The pages of the book Mathtopia are numbered from 1. The page numbers have a total of 459 digits. How many pages does the book have?

A) 119 B) 189 C) 190 D) 215 E) 219

Solution. The number of digits used until page 99 is $9+90\cdot 2 = 189$. Then there are $459-189 = 270$ digits more to be used. In other words, there are $270/3 = 90$ pages more to go. Starting on page 100, the 90-th page is 189. The answer is $\boxed{B}$. □

Problem 7. How many three-digit numbers with all digits greater than zero and digit sum 11 are there?

A) 27 B) 33 C) 39 D) 45 E) None of the preceding

Solution. Let abc be a three-digit number with all digits greater than zero and digit sum 11. Then $1 \leq a,b,c \leq 9$ and $a+b+c = 11$. Notice that any (a,b,c) solution over positive integers for the equation satisfies the inequality. Thus, there are $C(11-1, 3-1) = C(10,2) = 45$ such solutions. The answer is $\boxed{D}$. □

Problem 8. The diagram shows four identical rectangles placed inside a square. The perimeter of each identical rectangle is 24, and the perimeter of the center square is 20. What is the sum of the areas of the outer rectangles (border area)?

A) 110
B) 120
C) 124
D) 136
E) None of the preceding

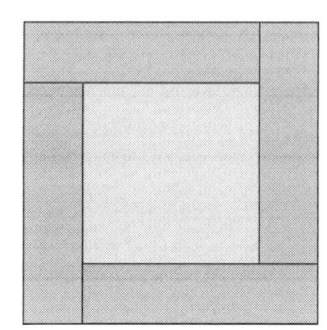

Solution. Since the perimeter of the center square is 20, each of its side lengths is 5. Now let the short side length of each identical rectangle be x. As shown in the figure on the right, the long side length is $5 + x$. Since the perimeter of each identical rectangle is 24, we have
$$2 \cdot (x + 5 + x) = 24.$$
That is, $x = \dfrac{7}{2}$. Then, the area of each rectangle is

$$\frac{7}{2} \cdot \left(5 + \frac{7}{2}\right) = \frac{119}{4}.$$

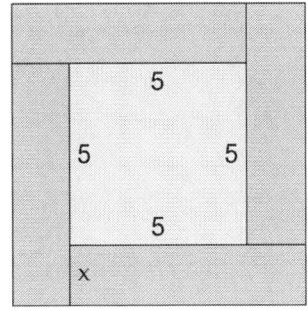

As there are four triangles, the sum of the areas of the outer rectangles is 119. The answer is $\boxed{E}$. □

Problem 9. If $2^{2018} - 2^{2017} - 2^{2016} + 2^{2015} = a \cdot 2^{2015}$, what is the value of a?

A) 3 B) 5 C) 8 D) 13 E) 16

Solution.
$$2^{2018} - 2^{2017} - 2^{2016} + 2^{2015} = (2^3 - 2^2 - 2 + 1) \cdot 2^{2015} = 3 \cdot 2^{2015}.$$
Therefore, $a = 3$. The answer is $\boxed{A}$. □

Problem 10. Let a and b be digits such that the eight-digit number aaaabbbb is a multiple of 45. What is the sum of all possible values of a?

A) 11 B) 13 C) 14 D) 15 E) 17

Solution. A number is a multiple of 45 if and only if it is divisible by 5 and 9. Then the unit digit b is either 0 or 5, and the sum of digits, i.e. $4a + 4b$, is divisible by 9. This is only possible when (a, b) is either $(9, 0)$ or $(4, 5)$. Thus, the sum of all possible values of a is $9 + 4 = 13$. The answer is $\boxed{B}$. □

Problem 11. A box has 6 red, 4 blue, and 7 green balls. How many balls must be drawn from the box to make sure that 1 red ball is selected?

A) 10 B) 11 C) 12 D) 13 E) 14

Solution. There are $4 + 7 = 11$ balls whose color is not red. Hence, one can draw 12 balls to guarantee that there is one red ball. The answer is $\boxed{C}$. □

Solutions for Practice Exam 5

Problem 12. Suppose ABCDEF is a regular hexagon with side length $2\sqrt{3}$. Find the area of $\triangle AEC$.

A) $9\sqrt{3}$

B) 12

C) $12\sqrt{2}$

D) $12\sqrt{3}$

E) None of the preceding

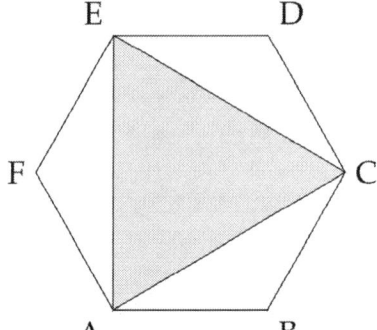

Solution. As $\triangle AFE$ is a 120-30-30 triangle, $AE = 2\sqrt{3} \cdot \sqrt{3} = 6$. Then $\triangle AEC$ is an equilateral triangle with side length 6. Thus, its area is $\dfrac{6^2 \sqrt{3}}{4} = 9\sqrt{3}$. The answer is $\boxed{A}$. □

Problem 13. How many integers n satisfy the compound inequality $\dfrac{1}{4} \leq \dfrac{n}{2019} \leq \dfrac{1}{3}$?

A) 150 B) 160 C) 167 D) 169 E) None of the preceding

Solution. Using the given inequality, we have $\dfrac{2019}{4} \leq n \leq \dfrac{2019}{3}$. Then, the possible values for n are $505, 506, \ldots, 673$. That is, there are $673 - 505 + 1 = 169$ integers. The answer is $\boxed{D}$. □

Problem 14. Let a and b are positive numbers such that $A = a^2 - b^2$ and A is a prime number. Which of the following would be the value of $a + b$?

A) 15 B) 23 C) 33 D) 45 E) 91

Solution. As $A = a^2 - b^2 = (a-b)(a+b)$ and A is prime, we must have $a - b = 1$. Then, $A = a + b$ is a prime number. Among given choices, only the number in choice B is a prime number. In that case, $a = 12$ and $b = 11$. The answer is $\boxed{B}$. □

Problem 15. How many even positive integers have their digits in strictly increasing order, when read left-to-right? Two examples include 8 and 12456, but not 334.

A) 128 B) 170 C) 255 D) 256 E) 511

Solution. Suppose the number ends with the even digit k for $k = 2, 4, 6$ or 8. Then we choose a subset of $\{1, 2, \ldots, k - 1\}$ (including the empty set, in that case, the number is just k) and uniquely arrange them to form a number so that the digits are strictly increasing. Then there are 2^{k-1} numbers ending with k. Thus, the result is $2^1 + 2^3 + 2^5 + 2^7 = 170$. The answer is $\boxed{B}$. □

Solutions for Practice Exam 5

Problem 16. The line $ax - by = -9$ passes through the points $(-1, 3)$ and $(-3, 0)$. What is the value of $a + b$?

A) 5 B) 6 C) 7 D) 8 E) 9

Solution. As the given line passes through the points $(-1, 3)$ and $(-3, 0)$, we have the following equations:
$$a(-1) - b(3) = -9 \quad \text{and} \quad a(-3) - b(0) = -9.$$
That is,
$$-a - 3b = -9 \quad \text{and} \quad -3a = -9.$$
Then we have $a = 3$ from the second equation, and therefore $b = 2$ from the first equation. Thus, $a + b = 5$. The answer is $\boxed{A}$. □

Problem 17. If $x = \dfrac{\sqrt{13} - 1}{\sqrt{3} + 1}$, then find the value of the expression $\dfrac{\sqrt{3} - 1}{\sqrt{13} + 1}$ in terms of x.

A) $\dfrac{x}{3}$ B) $\dfrac{x}{6}$ C) $\dfrac{x}{9}$ D) $\dfrac{2}{x}$ E) $\dfrac{6}{x}$

Solution. Let $y = \dfrac{\sqrt{3} - 1}{\sqrt{13} + 1}$. Then we have
$$\frac{x}{y} = \frac{\sqrt{13} - 1}{\sqrt{3} + 1} \cdot \frac{\sqrt{13} + 1}{\sqrt{3} - 1} = \frac{13 - 1}{3 - 1} = 6.$$
Thus $y = \dfrac{x}{6}$. The answer is $\boxed{B}$. □

Problem 18. N is the number $111\ldots 11$ formed by writing 105 ones in a row. What is the sum of the digits of the product $105 \times N$?

A) 612 B) 621 C) 630 D) 639 E) 648

Solution. Notice that
$$105 \times N = 100 \times N + 5 \times N = \underbrace{111\ldots 11}_{105 \text{ digits}} 00 + \underbrace{555\ldots 55}_{105 \text{ digits}} = 11\underbrace{666\ldots 66}_{103 \text{ digits}} 55.$$
Then, the sum of the digits of the result is $1 + 1 + 103 \times 6 + 5 + 5 = 630$. The answer is $\boxed{C}$. □

Problem 19. In how many ways can three different integers be selected from 1 to 10 such that no two integers chosen are consecutive?

A) 30 B) 56 C) 120 D) 360 E) 720

Solutions for Practice Exam 5

Solution. Consider 10 counters (X). We will arrange them in a row so each number between 1 to 10 is represented by the position of an X. Firstly, take away 3 of them, now 7 are left. Since there are 8 gaps, including ends, we can insert back the 3 so that no two of them are consecutive:

$$\_X\_X\_X\_X\_X\_X\_X\_$$

Thus, there are $C(8,3) = 56$ ways to choose three gaps for three X's. The answer is $\boxed{B}$. □

Problem 20. Suppose ABC is a right triangle with $\overline{AB} \perp \overline{AC}$ and $AB = AC = 20$. A point D is given inside $\triangle ABC$ such that $\overline{AD} \perp \overline{BD}$ and $BD = 16$. What is the area of $\triangle BCD$?

A) 24

B) 28

C) 30

D) 32

E) 36

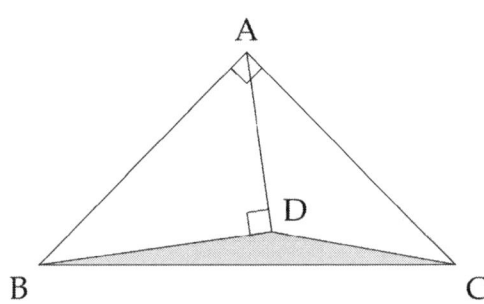

Solution. The area of $\triangle ABC$ is $\dfrac{20 \cdot 20}{2} = 200$. Since $\triangle ADB$ is a right triangle, $AD = 12$ by the Pythagorean theorem. Then, the area of $\triangle ABD$ is

$$\frac{12 \cdot 16}{2} = 96.$$

Suppose $m\angle DBA = \alpha$. As $\triangle ADB$ is a right triangle, we have

$$\sin \alpha = \frac{12}{20} = \frac{3}{5}.$$

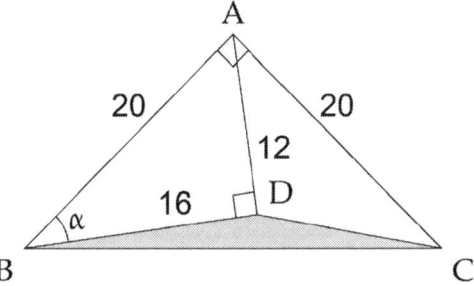

Moreover, $m\angle DAC = \alpha$. Using the sine law for the area of a triangle, we have that the area of $\triangle ADC$ is

$$\frac{1}{2}(12)(20)(\sin \alpha) = \frac{1}{2}(12)(20)\left(\frac{3}{5}\right) = 72.$$

Thus, the area of $\triangle BDC$ is $200 - (96 + 72) = 32$. The answer is $\boxed{D}$. □

Problem 21. If $x, y, -\dfrac{1}{2}$ is an arithmetic progression and $4, x, y$ is a geometric progression, then what is the value of $x + y$?

A) $\dfrac{6}{5}$ 　　B) $\dfrac{5}{4}$ 　　C) $\dfrac{5}{3}$ 　　D) 5 　　E) None of the preceding

Solutions for Practice Exam 5

Solution. As $x, y, -\frac{1}{2}$ is an arithmetic progression and $4, x, y$ is a geometric progression, we have
$$y = \frac{x - \frac{1}{2}}{2} \quad \text{and} \quad x = \sqrt{4 \cdot y},$$
respectively. That is,
$$x = 2y + \frac{1}{2} = \sqrt{4y}.$$
Then $y = \frac{1}{4}$ and so $x = 1$. Thus, $x + y = \frac{5}{4}$. The answer is $\boxed{B}$. □

Problem 22. Suppose p is a prime number, x is a positive integer, and n is a non-negative integer. For how many (x, n, p) do we have $n^2 p < 100$ and $n^2 + \frac{50x}{p} = (n + x)^2$?

A) 13 B) 14 C) 15 D) 16 E) 17

Solution. From the second equation, we have
$$n^2 + \frac{50x}{p} = (n+x)^2 \implies x^2 + 2nx - \frac{50x}{p} = 0 \implies x\left(x + 2n - \frac{50}{p}\right) = 0 \implies x = \frac{50}{p} - 2n.$$
As x is an integer, p divides 50. That is, p is either 2 or 5 since p is prime. If $p = 2$, we have
$$n^2 < 50 \quad \text{and} \quad x = 25 - 2n.$$
Hence the solutions when $p = 2$ are (25, 0, 2), (23, 1, 2), (21, 2, 2), (19, 3, 2), (17, 4, 2), (15, 5, 2), (13, 6, 2) and (11, 7, 2). On the other hand, if $p = 5$, we have
$$n^2 < 20 \quad \text{and} \quad x = 10 - 2n.$$
Hence the solutions for $p = 5$ are (10, 0, 5), (8, 1, 5), (6, 2, 5), (4, 3, 5) and (2, 4, 5). Therefore, there are 13 solutions. The answer is $\boxed{A}$. □

Problem 23. A coin is weighted so that it has probability p of landing heads and probability $1 - p$ of landing tails, where $0 < p < 1$. If this coin is flipped twice, the probability that two heads are obtained is exactly twice the probability that exactly one head is obtained. What is p?

A) $\frac{1}{2}$ B) $\frac{2}{3}$ C) $\frac{3}{4}$ D) $\frac{4}{5}$ E) $\frac{5}{6}$

Solution. The probability that two heads are obtained is p^2. On the other hand, the probability that exactly one head is obtained is $2(p)(1-p) = 2p - 2p^2$. Then, when we solve
$$p^2 = 2(2p - 2p^2),$$
we get $p = \frac{4}{5}$. The answer is $\boxed{D}$. □

153

Solutions for Practice Exam 5

Problem 24. ABC is an isosceles triangle with $AB = AC = 5$ and $BC = 8$. Point P is inside $\triangle ABC$ such that the product of the area of $\triangle APB$, the area of $\triangle APC$, and the area of $\triangle BPC$ is maximum. What is the value of PB?

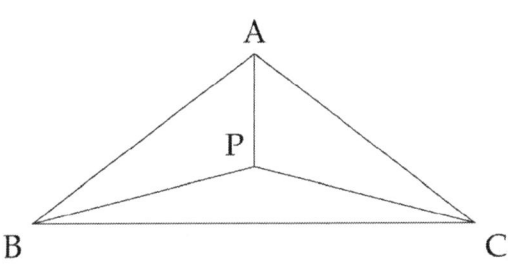

A) 3

B) $\sqrt{10}$

C) $2\sqrt{3}$

D) $\sqrt{17}$

E) $2\sqrt{5}$

Solution. Let h be the height from P to $\overline{BC}$ with $\overline{PD} \perp \overline{BC}$. Notice that the area of $\triangle ABC$ is $\sqrt{9 \cdot 4 \cdot 4 \cdot 1} = 12$ by Heron's formula. Then,

Area $(\triangle PAB)$ + Area $(\triangle PAC)$ + Area $(\triangle PBC) = 12$.

To maximize their product, we should have

Area $(\triangle PAB)$ = Area $(\triangle PAC)$ = Area $(\triangle PBC) = 4$.

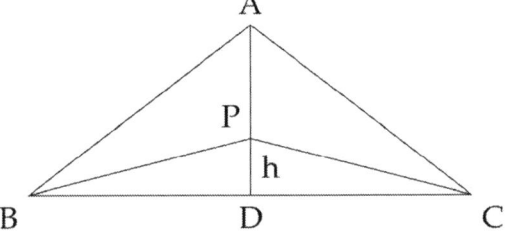

On the other hand, as Area $(\triangle PAB)$ = Area $(\triangle PAC)$, we have $m\angle PAB = m\angle PAC$, and therefore $PB = PC$. Thus, $\triangle PBC$ is an isosceles triangle and so $BD = DC = 4$. Thus, $PB = \sqrt{4^2 + 1^2} = \sqrt{17}$. The answer is $\boxed{D}$. □

Problem 25. A mathematician offers you the following game. He will flip 10 fair coins, and if n coins land heads, then you win n^2 dollars (for example, if 4 coins land heads, then you win $16, and if 0 coins land heads, then you win $0). How many dollars should the mathematician charge to play the game so that the game is fair?

Note: A game is *fair* if the expected profit after playing the game is zero.

A) $25   B) $27.50   C) $28   D) $28.50   E) $30

Solution. Suppose the player is charged x dollars. We can draw the following probability table with respect to the number of heads:

154

Solutions for Practice Exam 6

Number of heads (N)	Win ($ N²)	Probability (C(10, N)/2^{10})
0	$ 0	$1/2^{10}$
1	$ 1	$10/2^{10}$
2	$ 4	$45/2^{10}$
3	$ 9	$120/2^{10}$
4	$ 16	$210/2^{10}$
5	$ 25	$252/2^{10}$
6	$ 36	$210/2^{10}$
7	$ 49	$120/2^{10}$
8	$ 64	$45/2^{10}$
9	$ 81	$10/2^{10}$
10	$ 100	$1/2^{10}$

Using the expected value formula, we have

$$x = \sum_{N=0}^{10} (N^2)(C(10,N)/2^{10}) = 0 \cdot \frac{1}{2^{10}} + 1 \cdot \frac{10}{2^{10}} + 4 \cdot \frac{45}{2^{10}} + \ldots + 100 \cdot \frac{1}{2^{10}} = 27.5$$

The answer is $\boxed{B}$. □

Solutions for Practice Exam 6

Problem 1. The length of a string is x. When two other strings, one of which is twice as long and the other three times as long, are connected to the original string at the right and the left ends respectively, the midpoint of these three strings altogether is 6 feet to the left of the mid-point of the original string. Which is the value of x?

A) 12 feet   B) 15 feet   C) 18 feet   D) 24 feet   E) 32 feet

Solution. Let x be the length of the original string. Then a string of length 3x is added to left end and a string of length 2x is added to right end. Since $3x > 2x$, the midpoint of the new string is $\frac{3x - 2x}{2} = \frac{x}{2}$ to the left of the midpoint of the original string. Since this value is 6 feet, we have $x = 12$ feet. The answer is $\boxed{A}$. □

Problem 2. Suppose x is a positive integer and the number $45 \cdot x$ is made of the digits "0" and "6". What is the sum of all digits of the minimum possible value of x?

A) 9   B) 10   C) 11   D) 12   E) 13

Solution. The number $45 \cdot x$ is divisible by both 5 and 9. Therefore, the units digit is "0" and the sum of its digits is divisible by 9. On the other hand, since the minimum multiple of 6 that is divisible by 9 is $3 \cdot 6 = 18$, there are three "6" digits used. Then, the minimum value of $45 \cdot x$

Solutions for Practice Exam 6

with three "6"'s and "0" in the units is 6660. Thus, $x = \dfrac{6660}{45} = 148$ and therefore the result is $1 + 4 + 8 = 13$. The answer is $\boxed{E}$. □

Problem 3. Nine points are equally spaced around the circumference of a circle. How many non-equilateral triangles can be formed by choosing three of these nine points as vertices of the triangle?

A) 42 B) 72 C) 75 D) 81 E) 84

Solution. Let $A_1, A_2, \ldots, A_9$ be such points on the circle. There are $C(9,3) = 84$ triangles. Among them, the equilateral triangles are $A_1A_4A_7$, $A_2A_5A_8$, $A_3A_6A_9$. Therefore, there are $84 - 3 = 81$ non-equilateral triangles. The answer is $\boxed{D}$. □

Problem 4. ABCD is a quadrilateral and E is a point on ABCD such that $\overline{AE}$ and $\overline{DE}$ are angle bisectors of $\angle BAD$ and $\angle ADC$, respectively. What is the value of m$\angle$AED?

A) 60°
B) 75°
C) 90°
D) 100°
E) None of the preceding

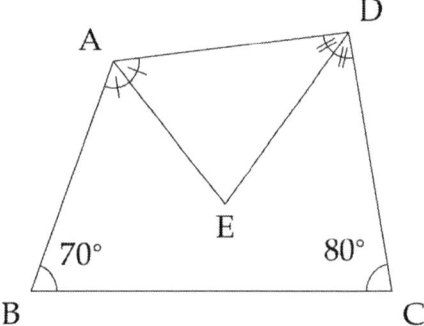

Solution. Let m$\angle$BAE = α and m$\angle$CDE = β. Then, we have
$$360° = 2\alpha + 2\beta + 70° + 80°.$$
That is, $\alpha + \beta = 105°$. Therefore,
$$m\angle AED = 180° - (\alpha + \beta) = 180° - 105° = 75°.$$
The answer is $\boxed{B}$. □

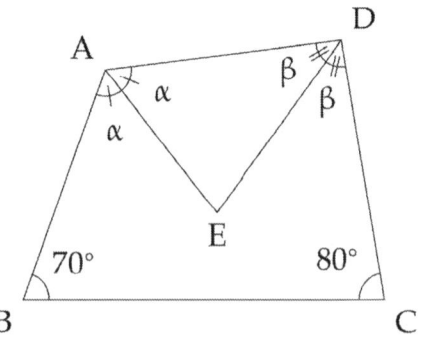

Problem 5. The arithmetic mean of X and Y is 12, the arithmetic mean of X and Z is 6, and the arithmetic mean of Y and Z is 4. What is the value of Z?

Solutions for Practice Exam 6

A) −5   B) −2   C) 6   D) 10   E) 12

Solution. Using the arithmetic means given in the question, we have

$$X + Y + Z = \frac{X+Y}{2} + \frac{X+Z}{2} + \frac{Y+Z}{2} = 12 + 6 + 4 = 22.$$

Then,

$$Z = 22 - (X + Y) = 22 - 2 \cdot \left(\frac{X+Y}{2}\right) = 22 - 2 \cdot 12 = -2.$$

The answer is $\boxed{B}$. □

Problem 6. Suppose a and b are positive integers and $a^2 - b^2$ is a prime number. Which of the following is always correct?

A) $ab = a + b - 1$

B) $ab = a + b + 1$

C) $a^2 - b^2 = 2$

D) $(a - b)^2 = a + b - 2$

E) $a - b = 1$

Solution. Notice that $a^2 - b^2 = (a - b)(a + b)$. Then $a^2 - b^2$ is a prime number if and only if $a - b = 1$ and $a + b$ is a prime number. In that case, it seems the choice E is always correct. For the other choices we can find a counter example, such as $a = 4$ and $b = 3$, to show that they are not always correct. The answer is $\boxed{E}$. □

Problem 7. For numbering the pages of a book, a total of 2933 digits are used. How many pages does this book have?

A) 1010   B) 1001   C) 1105   D) 1110   E) 1015

Solution. The number of digits used for the page numbers 1 to 9 is 9, for the page numbers 10 to 99 is $2 \cdot 90 = 180$, and for the page numbers 100 to 999 $3 \cdot 900 = 2700$. So there are $2993 - (2700 + 180 + 9) = 44$ digits left to be used for page numbering. It means there are $44/4 = 11$ pages more. Starting with the page 1000, we conclude that the book has 1010 pages in total. The answer is $\boxed{A}$. □

Problem 8. ABCD is a quadrilateral with $\overline{AB} \perp \overline{AD}$, $m\angle ABC = 45°$, $BC = 5\sqrt{2}$, $AD = 10$, and $AB = 17$. What is the value of CD?

Solutions for Practice Exam 6

A) $8\sqrt{2}$

B) 12

C) $9\sqrt{2}$

D) 13

E) None of the preceding

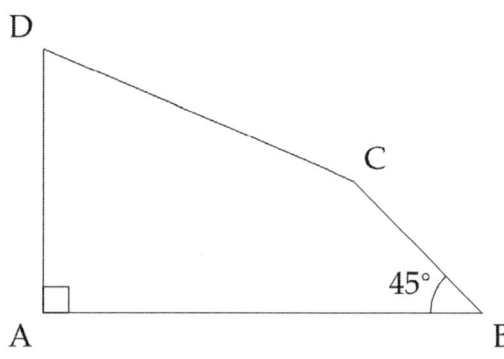

Solution. Let E and F be points on $\overline{AB}$ and $\overline{AD}$, respectively, such that $\overline{CE} \perp \overline{AB}$ and $\overline{CF} \perp \overline{AD}$. As $m\angle ABC = 45°$, we have that then $\triangle BEC$ is a right isosceles triangle, and therefore $BE = CE = 5$. Then $AE = AB - BE = 12$. As AECF is a rectangle, we also have $CF = 12$ and $AF = 5$. Then $DF = AD - AF = 5$. Finally, applying the Pythagorean theorem on $\triangle CDF$, we have $DC = 13$. The answer is $\boxed{D}$. □

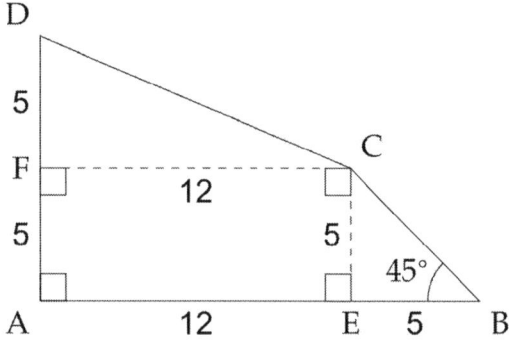

Problem 9. If x and y are positive whole numbers and $x + \dfrac{y^3}{5} = 26$, then what is the value of y?

A) 2 B) 3 C) 4 D) 5 E) 6

Solution. As $\dfrac{y^3}{5} = 26 - x$ is an integer, we first have $5|y^3$. However, 5 is a prime number, so $5|y$. That is, there exists some $k \in \mathbb{N}$ such that $y = 5k$. Hence, $y^3 = 125k^3 = 130 - 5x$. The only possible solution of this equation for positive integers x and k is $x = 1$ and $k = 1$. Thus $y = 5$. The answer is $\boxed{D}$. □

Problem 10. For how many distinct integer values of n is $\dfrac{n^2}{n+4}$ also an integer?

A) 4 B) 5 C) 8 D) 10 E) 12

Solution. Assume $\dfrac{n^2}{n+4}$ is an integer. Then

$$(n+4)|n^2 = n^2 - 16 + 16 = (n+4)(n-4) + 16$$

must hold. So $(n+4)$ divides 16. Thus the possible values for $n+4$ are $\pm 1, \pm 2, \pm 4, \pm 8, \pm 16$, that is, there are 10 possible integer values for n. The answer is $\boxed{D}$. □

Solutions for Practice Exam 6

Problem 11. There are 5 students in a math team, and 2 chaperones join them at a math competition. They pose for a group photo and sit in 5 chairs arranged in a line. The photographer requests that there be exactly two students between the chaperones. How many ways can they be arranged for the photo?

A) 120   B) 240   C) 360   D) 480   E) 960

Solution. This is possible in two cases: CSSCS or SCSSC. Thus, there are

$$2 \cdot P(5,3) \cdot P(2,2) = 2 \cdot 60 \cdot 2 = 240$$

arrangements. The answer is $\boxed{B}$.

Problem 12. A rectangular sheet of paper is placed on top of another as shown with $AB = 3$, $DE = 2$, $BI = 6$, and $DG = 9$. The dimensions of the larger sheet are double those of the smaller sheet. What is the total shaded area?

A) 96
B) 102
C) 106
D) 110
E) 114

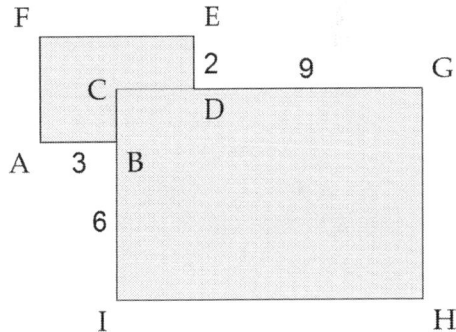

Solution. As shown in the following figure, we have

$$2(x+2) = x+6 \implies x = 2,$$

and

$$2(y+3) = y+9 \implies y = 3.$$

Therefore, the dimensions of the rectangles are 4×6 and 8×12 with an overlapping rectangle of dimension 2×3. Thus, the shaded area is $4 \cdot 6 + 8 \cdot 12 - 2 \cdot 3 = 24 + 96 - 6 = 114$. The answer is $\boxed{E}$.

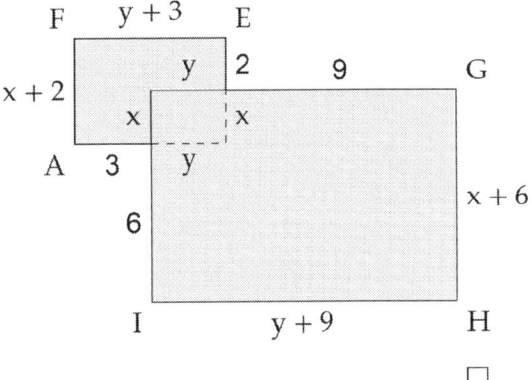

Problem 13. What is the value of n so that $(n + 3^{2019})^2 - (n - 3^{2019})^2 = 3^{2019} + 3^{2020}$?

A) 1   B) 9   C) 3^{2019} D) 3^{2020} E) 3^{2038}

Solutions for Practice Exam 6

Solution. Notice that $3^{2019} + 3^{2020} = (1+3) \cdot 3^{2019} = 4 \cdot 3^{2019}$. On the other hand,

$$(n + 3^{2019})^2 - (n - 3^{2019})^2 = (n + 3^{2019} + n - 3^{2019}) \cdot (n + 3^{2019} - n + 3^{2019})$$
$$= (2n)(2 \cdot 3^{2019})$$
$$= 4n \cdot 3^{2019}$$

Thus, $n = 1$. The answer is $\boxed{A}$. $\square$

Problem 14. How many positive integers not exceeding 2017 are multiples of 3 or 4 but not 5?

    A) 792   B) 807   C) 917   D) 927   E) None

Solution. Define the sets

$$A = \{1 \leq x \leq 2017 \text{ and } 3|x\},$$
$$B = \{1 \leq x \leq 2017 \text{ and } 4|x\},$$
$$C = \{1 \leq x \leq 2017 \text{ and } 5|x\}.$$

Then

$$|(A \cup B) \ C| = |A| + |B| - |A \cap B| - |A \cap C| - |B \cap C| + |A \cap B \cap C|$$
$$= \left\lfloor \frac{2017}{3} \right\rfloor + \left\lfloor \frac{2017}{4} \right\rfloor - \left\lfloor \frac{2017}{12} \right\rfloor - \left\lfloor \frac{2017}{15} \right\rfloor - \left\lfloor \frac{2017}{20} \right\rfloor + \left\lfloor \frac{2017}{60} \right\rfloor$$
$$= 672 + 504 - 168 - 134 - 100 + 33$$
$$= 807$$

The answer is $\boxed{B}$. $\square$

Problem 15. In how many ways can 9 different red and 6 different white balls be arranged in a row with no two white balls next to each other?

A) $P(10,9) \cdot 6!$

B) $C(10,9) \cdot 6!$

C) $P(10,6) \cdot 9!$

D) $P(10,9) \cdot 6!$

E) None of the preceding

Solution. There are 10 spaces among 9 red balls to place 6 white balls into those spaces. When we permute 6 white balls into those spaces separately, no two of them are next to each other. Thus, the answer is $P(10,6) \cdot 9!$. The answer is $\boxed{C}$. $\square$

Solutions for Practice Exam 6

Problem 16. What is the area of the triangle formed by the lines $y = 6 - x$, $y = 6 + x$, and $y = 2$?

A) 16 B) 18 C) 19 D) 20 E) 21

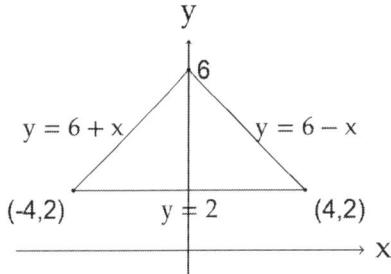

Solution. The intersection points are $(2, 4)$, $(2, -4)$ and $(0, 6)$. As drawn in the figure on the right, the height is 4 and the length of the base is 8 in the triangle. Therefore, its area is $\frac{4 \cdot 8}{2} = 16$. The answer is $\boxed{A}$. □

Problem 17. Patrick, the master gardener, has 100 lbs of tomatoes that were 90% water by weight. He dried the tomatoes in the sun until they were 80% water by weight. How much do Partick's sun-dried tomatoes weigh? Round your answer to the nearest 10 lbs.

A) 50 B) 60 C) 65 D) 70 E) 75

Solution. In the beginning, the weight of the water was $0.90 \cdot 100 = 90$ lbs. Suppose x lbs of water evaporated after sun drying. Then $0.80 \cdot (100 - x) = 90 - x$. That is, $x = 50$. Therefore, the weight of the sun-dried tomatoes is 100 lbs − 50 lbs = 50 lbs. The answer is $\boxed{A}$. □

Problem 18. The product of two prime numbers is one less than a perfect square. Given that both prime numbers are less than 100, what is the largest possible value of one of these primes?

A) 73 B) 79 C) 83 D) 89 E) 97

Solution. Let p and q be prime numbers with $p < q$ and $pq = a^2 - 1$ for some positive integer a. Then $pq = (a-1)(a+1)$, that is, $p = a - 1$ and $q = a + 1$. The largest pair (p, q) with $p < q < 100$ is $(71, 73)$. The answer is $\boxed{A}$. □

Problem 19. Two cards are dealt from a standard deck of 52 playing cards, without replacement. What is the probability that the cards are of the same suit?

A) $\frac{1}{17}$ B) $\frac{3}{17}$ C) $\frac{4}{17}$ D) $\frac{3}{13}$ E) $\frac{1}{4}$

Solution. Notice that there are 13 cards in each suit. Therefore, the number of pairs of the same suit are $4 \cdot C(13, 2) = 312$. In total, two cards can be chosen in $C(52, 2) = 1326$ ways. Then the probability is $\frac{312}{1326} = \frac{4}{17}$. The answer is $\boxed{C}$. □

Solutions for Practice Exam 6

Problem 20. △ABC is an isosceles triangle with AB = AC and m∠BAC = 120°. The points F and G are the midpoints of $\overline{AB}$ and $\overline{AC}$ respectively. The points D and E are on $\overline{BC}$ such that $\overline{DF} \perp \overline{AB}$ and $\overline{EG} \perp \overline{AC}$. If BC = 24, what is the area of FGED?

A) 20 B) $20\sqrt{3}$ C) 24 D) 32 E) 40

Solution. FGDE is a trapezoid with height $2\sqrt{3}$. Thus, the area of FGDE is

$$\frac{(12+8) \cdot 2\sqrt{3}}{2} = 20\sqrt{3}.$$

The answer is $\boxed{B}$. □

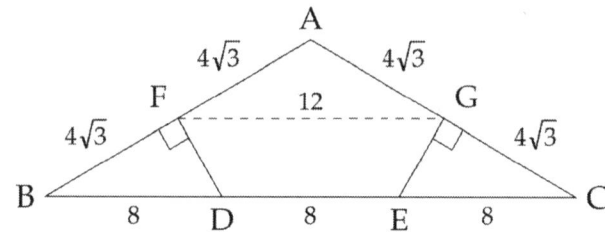

Problem 21. How many pairs (x, y) of real numbers satisfy the following system of equations?

$$x^2 + xy = 2y^2 \quad \text{and} \quad y^2 - xy = 1$$

A) 0 B) 1 C) 2 D) 3 E) None of the preceding

Solution. From the first equation, $x^2 + xy - 2y^2 = (x-y)(x+2y) = 0$. That is, either $x = y$ or $x = -2y$. If $x = y$, the second equation is transformed into $0 = 1$, which is not possible. If $x = -2y$, the second equation is transformed into $3y^2 = 1$, i.e. $y = \pm 1/\sqrt{3}$. Thus, the solutions are $(-2/\sqrt{3}, 1/\sqrt{3})$ and $(2/\sqrt{3}, -1/\sqrt{3})$. The answer is $\boxed{C}$. □

Problem 22. Let T(n) be the digit sum of a positive integer n. For example, $T(5081) = 5 + 0 + 8 + 1 = 14$. How many positive three-digit numbers n satisfy $T(n) + 3n = 2020$?

A) 0 B) 1 C) 2 D) 3 E) 4

Solution. Let n = abc be a three-digit number. Then

$$2020 = T(n) + 3n = (a+b+c) + 3 \cdot (100a + 10b + c) = 301a + 31b + 4c.$$

We have that $301a \leq 2020$, that is, $a \leq 6$. On the other hand,

$$2020 - 301a = 31b + 4c \leq 31 \cdot 9 + 4 \cdot 9 = 315,$$

that is, $a \geq 6$. Combining these two inequalities related to a, we have $a = 6$. Then, we have $31b + 4c = 214$. A similar analysis gives that $c = 6$ and $b = 7$. Thus, there is only one solution $(a,b,c) = (6,6,7)$. The answer is $\boxed{B}$.

Solutions for Practice Exam 6

Alternative Solution. Notice that $n \equiv T(n) \pmod 9$. Therefore,

$$2020 = T(n) + 3n \equiv 4 \cdot T(n) \pmod 9.$$

Since $2020 \equiv 4 \pmod 9$, we have $T(n) \equiv 1 \pmod 9$. Moreover, we know that $1 \leq T(n) \leq 27$ since n is a three-digit number. Then, the possible values for $T(n)$ are 1, 10 and 19. First two values $T(n) = 1$ and $T(n) = 10$ are not possible because they imply $n = 673$ and $n = 670$, respectively. But $T(n) = 19$ implies $n = 667$, which is consistent. Thus, there is only one solution. □

Problem 23. As shown in the figure, 12 points are chosen on a 4×7 grid. How many different right triangles can be drawn using these points?

A) 28

B) 29

C) 30

D) 31

E) 32

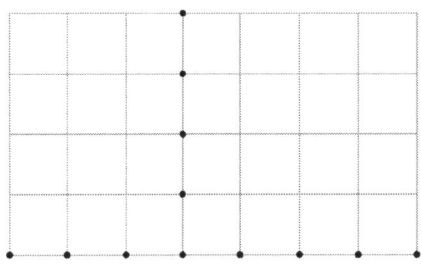

Solution. Label the points as shown in the figure. Notice that the right angle occurs at one of the points b_0, b_1, b_2, b_3 and b_4. If the right angle occurs at b_0, then we choose one point from $\{b_1, b_2, b_3, b_4\}$ and another point from $\{a_0, a_1, a_2, a_3, a_4, a_5, a_6\}$ to construct a right triangle. In this way, we can construct $4 \cdot 7 = 28$ right triangles.

However, if the right angle occurs at one of the points b_1, b_2, b_3 and b_4, then the possible right triangles are constructed by choosing (b_1, a_2, a_3), (b_2, a_1, a_4), (b_2, a_2, a_6), or (b_3, a_0, a_5). Thus, we have 4 right triangles more.

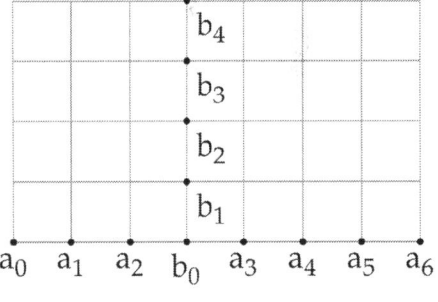

In total, there are 32 right triangles. The answer is $\boxed{E}$.
□

Problem 24. In $\triangle ABC$, the medians $\overline{BE}$ and $\overline{CD}$ intersect at the point G so that $\overline{BE} \perp \overline{CD}$. If $BE = 18$ and $CD = 24$, what is the value of AG?

A) 15   B) 20   C) 25   D) 30   E) None of the preceding

Solutions for Practice Exam 6

Solution. Draw the median $\overline{AF}$ as well. Notice that the point G is the centroid of $\triangle ABC$. Therefore, it divides each median in the ratio $2:1$. That is, $BG = 12$ and $CG = 16$. Since $\triangle CGB$ is a right triangle and $\overline{FG}$ is one of its medians, we have

$$FG = CF = BF = \frac{BC}{2}.$$

As $BC = \sqrt{16^2 + 12^2} = 20$ by the Pythagorean theorem, we have

$$AG = 2GF = BC = 20.$$

The answer is $\boxed{B}$. □

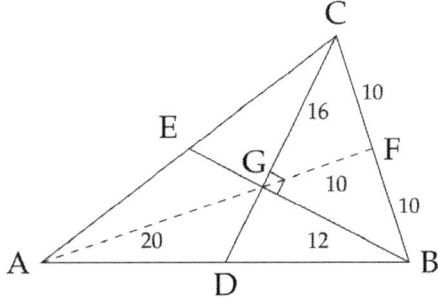

Problem 25. ABCD is a parallelogram. The points E and F are on $\overline{CD}$ and $\overline{BC}$, respectively, such that $BF = FC$ and $CE = 3ED$. The points H and G are such that $\overleftrightarrow{BE} \cap \overleftrightarrow{AD} = G$ and $\overleftrightarrow{BE} \cap \overleftrightarrow{AF} = H$. If $BH : HE : EG = a : b : c$ for some positive integers a, b and c, what is the minimum value of $a + b + c$?

A) 21
B) 36
C) 40
D) 44
E) 48

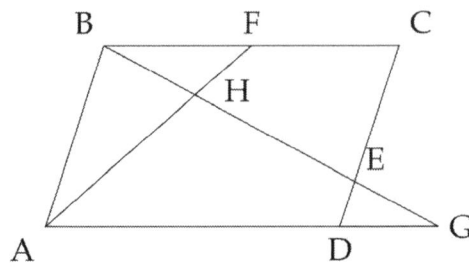

Solution. Let $ED = y$ and $DG = 2x$. Using the "Bow-Tie" similarity from the point E (i.e. $\triangle EDG \sim \triangle ECB$), we have

$$EC = 3y, \quad BC = 6x, \quad \frac{c}{a+b} = \frac{1}{3}.$$

Using the "Bow-Tie" similarity from the point H (i.e. $\triangle BHF \sim \triangle GHA$), we have

$$\frac{a}{b+c} = \frac{3x}{8x} = \frac{3}{8}.$$

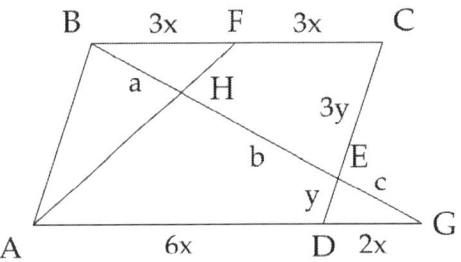

Thus, $a = 12k$, $b = 21k$ and $c = 11k$ for some positive integer k. Therefore, the minimum value of $a + b + c$ is 44. The answer is $\boxed{D}$. □

Solutions for Practice Exam 7

Problem 1. The car with speed 40 mph travels from Arlington Heights to Mt. Prospect and with speed 60 mph from Mt. Prospect to Arlington Heights. Which of the following is the average speed of the car for the entire trip?

A) 48   B) 49   C) 50   D) 51   E) 52

Solution. Let x be the distance between Arlington Heights and Mt. Prospect in miles. Then it takes $\frac{x}{40}$ hours to go from Arlington Heights to Mt. Prospect, and $\frac{x}{60}$ hours to go from Mt. Prospect to Arlington Heights. Since the total distance that the car travels is 2x, the average speed of the car is

$$\frac{2x}{\frac{x}{40} + \frac{x}{60}} = \frac{2x}{5x/120} = \frac{240}{5} = 48 \text{ miles.}$$

The answer is $\boxed{A}$. □

Problem 2. A 500 page book is numbered consecutively, starting with 1. How many times does the digit 1 appear in the page numbers?

A) 150   B) 160   C) 180   D) 190   E) 200

Solution. Up to page 99, it appears on pages $1, 10, 11, 12, \ldots, 19, 21, 31, \ldots, 91$. That is, it appears 20 times. In the pages 1xy, it appears $100 + 20 = 120$ times. In the pages 2xy, 3xy and 4xy, it appears $3 \cdot 20 = 60$ times. Thus, it appears 200 times in total. The answer is $\boxed{E}$. □

Solutions for Practice Exam 7

Problem 3. Raj rolls a standard 6-sided die. Sena rolls a second 6-sided die. Raj wins if the values shown differ by 1. What is the probability that Sena loses?

A) $\frac{1}{3}$ B) $\frac{2}{9}$ C) $\frac{1}{6}$ D) $\frac{5}{18}$ E) $\frac{7}{36}$

Solution. Let (a,b) denotes the numbers on the dice. There are 36 tuples in total. However, we are looking for tuples where Raj wins. That is, $|a-b| = 1$. Such tuples are $(1,2)$, $(2,1)$, $(2,3)$, $(3,2)$, $(3,4)$, $(4,3)$, $(4,5)$, $(5,4)$, $(5,6)$, and $(6,5)$. In other words, there are 10 tuples where Raj wins. Thus, the probability that Sena loses is $\frac{10}{36} = \frac{5}{18}$. The answer is $\boxed{D}$. □

Problem 4. One side of a triangle has length 6.3 and another side has length 1.7. How many integer values are possible for the length of the third side?

A) 1   B) 2   C) 3   D) 4   E) 5

Solution. Let x be the third side length. Using triangle inequality, $6.3 + 1.7 > x > 6.3 - 1.7$. That is, $8 > x > 4.6$. So the possible integer values for x are 7, 6 and 5. The answer is $\boxed{C}$.   □

Problem 5. If $A = \sqrt{\frac{1}{16} - \frac{1}{25}}$ and $B = \sqrt{\frac{1}{16}} - \sqrt{\frac{1}{25}}$, then what is the value of $\frac{A}{B}$?

A) 1   B) 3   C) 6   D) 8   E) None

Solution. We have
$$A = \sqrt{\frac{1}{16} - \frac{1}{25}} = \sqrt{\frac{25-16}{400}} = \frac{3}{20}$$
and
$$B = \sqrt{\frac{1}{16}} - \sqrt{\frac{1}{25}} = \frac{1}{4} - \frac{1}{5} = \frac{1}{20}$$
Thus $\frac{A}{B} = 3$. The answer is $\boxed{B}$.   □

Problem 6. How many integers from 2 to 99 inclusive have at least one digit that is a prime number?

A) 72   B) 64   C) 48   D) 36   E) 18

Solution. Notice that the prime digits are 2, 3, 5 and 7. Using the remaining non-prime digits, we can write $6 \times 6 - 2 = 34$ numbers between 2 and 99 (by excluding 0 and 1). As there are 98 numbers in total, $98 - 34 = 64$ numbers contain at least one digit that is a prime number. The answer is $\boxed{B}$.   □

Solutions for Practice Exam 7

Problem 7. The acute angles of an obtuse triangle measure a° and b°. If both of a and b are prime numbers, what is the maximum value of a + b?

A) 86   B) 87   C) 88   D) 89   E) None of the preceding

Solution. We are given that a° + b° < 90°. Notice that if a + b is odd, then either a or b is 2. However, it is not possible to have a + b = 89 because 87 is not prime. On the other hand, there are many candidates satisfying a + b = 88, such as (5, 83), (17, 71), (29, 59), (41, 47) and their symmetries. The answer is $\boxed{C}$. □

Problem 8. ABC is an isosceles triangle with AB = BC. D is a point inside △ABC such that AD = DC. If m∠ABC = 50° and m∠ADC = 130°, what is the value of m∠BAD =?

A) 35°   B) 40°   C) 45°   D) 50°   E) 55°

Solution. Let H be the foot of the altitude from B to $\overline{AC}$. As AD = DC, the point D is on $\overline{BH}$. Since $\overline{BH}$ is also the bisector of ∠ABC, we have m∠ABH = m∠HBC = 25°. Similarly, we have m∠ADH = m∠HDC = 65°. Thus,

$$m\angle BAD = m\angle BAC - m\angle DAC = 40°.$$

The answer is $\boxed{B}$. □

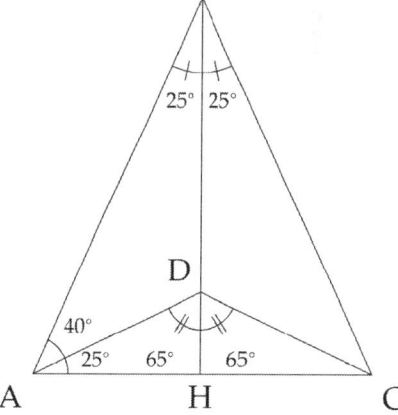

Problem 9. Half of a stick is divided into 14 equal parts and the other half of the stick is divided into 9 equal parts. The difference between one of the longer parts and one of the shorter parts measures 10 units. What is the total length of the stick?

A) 252   B) 378   C) 420   D) 500   E) 504

Solution. Let x be the total length of the stick. Then the length of each longer part is $\frac{(x/2)}{9} = \frac{x}{18}$, and the length of each shorter part is $\frac{(x/2)}{14} = \frac{x}{28}$. Since their length differ by 10 units, that is,

$$\frac{x}{18} - \frac{x}{28} = 10,$$

we have x = 504. The answer is $\boxed{E}$. □

Solutions for Practice Exam 7

Problem 10. For how many different values of C is 27C4 divisible by 6?

A) 0   B) 1   C) 2   D) 3   E) 4

Solution. 27C4 is divisible by 6 if and only if it is divisible by 2 and 3. It is obviously divisible by 2 because it is even. It is divisible by 3 if and only if $2 + 7 + C + 4 = 13 + C$ is divisible by 3. Thus, the possible values of C are 2, 5 and 8. The answer is $\boxed{D}$. □

Problem 11. How many three-digit numbers are even but have exactly one odd digit?

A) 100   B) 125   C) 200   D) 225   E) None of the preceding

Solution. A three digit number abc is even if and only if c is even. So one of a or b is odd. If a is odd, then there are $5 \cdot 5 \cdot 5 = 125$ such numbers. Otherwise, if a is even, there are $4 \cdot 5 \cdot 5 = 100$ such numbers. Hence, there are 225 such numbers in total. The answer is $\boxed{D}$. □

Problem 12. The sides of a triangle have lengths 7, 14, and c, where c is an integer. For how many values of c is the triangle acute?

A) 2   B) 3   C) 4   D) 5   E) 8

Solution. The triangle is acute if

$$\sqrt{14^2 + 7^2} > c > |14 - 7|, \quad \sqrt{c^2 + 7^2} > 14 > |7 - c|, \quad \text{and } \sqrt{c^2 + 14^2} > 7 > |14 - c|$$

hold. This is possible when $c = 13, 14$ or 15. That is, there are 3 such acute triangles. The answer is $\boxed{B}$. □

Problem 13. If $5^2 + 5^3 + ... + 5^{20} = M$, then what is the value of $5^2 + 5^3 + ... + 5^{18}$?

A) $M + 19$ B) $M - 5^{21}$ C) $\dfrac{M - 150}{25}$ D) $\dfrac{M - 36}{9}$ E) $\dfrac{M}{25}$

Solution.

$$5^2 + 5^3 + ... + 5^{20} = M \implies 5^4 + 5^5 ... + 5^{20} = M - 5^2 - 5^3 \implies 5^2 + 5^3 + ... + 5^{18} = \frac{M - 150}{25}.$$

The answer is $\boxed{C}$. □

Problem 14. What is the sum of all prime factors of $11^2 + 55^2$?

A) 16   B) 22   C) 23   D) 25   E) 26

Solutions for Practice Exam 7

Solution. We can factor 11^2 out. So, $11^2 + 55^2 = 11^2(1 + 5^2) = 11^2 \cdot 2 \cdot 13$. Thus, the sum of all prime factors $\Rightarrow 11 + 2 + 13 = 26$. The answer is $\boxed{E}$ □

Problem 15. Three tiles are marked A and two other tiles are marked B. The five tiles are randomly arranged in a row. What is the probability that the arrangement reads ABABA?

A) $\dfrac{1}{10}$ B) $\dfrac{1}{8}$ C) $\dfrac{1}{6}$ D) $\dfrac{1}{5}$ E) $\dfrac{1}{4}$

Solution. The number of arrangements of 3 A's and 2 B's is $C(5,3) = 10$. Thus, the probability is $\dfrac{1}{10}$. The answer is $\boxed{A}$. □

Problem 16. How many distinct isosceles triangles can be created with integer sides and a perimeter of 200 units?

A) 49 B) 64 C) 81 D) 96 E) None of the preceding

Solution. Let a, a, b be the side lengths of an isosceles triangle. We need to count the positive integer solutions (a, b) satisfying $2a + b = 200$. By the triangle inequality, we have $2a > b > 0$. Thus, $4a > 2a + b = 200$, that is, $a > 50$. Then, the solutions are $(51, 98), (52, 96), \ldots, (99, 2)$. In other words, we have 49 solutions. The answer is $\boxed{A}$. □

Problem 17. Mrs. Walker leaves for a walk at 11:00 am starting at point A. She walks from A to B on level ground, walks uphill from B to C, walks downhill from C to D, turns around, and then retraces her steps and returns to point A at 1:00 pm the same day. If her speed is four miles per hour on level ground, three miles per hour uphill, and six miles per hour downhill, how far does she walk in total?

A) 8 miles B) 9 miles C) 10 miles D) 12 miles E) 16 miles

Solution. Let x be the distance from point A to point B, y be the distance from point B to point C, and z be the distance from point C to point D. As she travelled for two hours in total, we have

$$2 \text{ hours} = \frac{x}{4 \text{ mph}} + \frac{y}{3 \text{ mph}} + \frac{z}{6 \text{ mph}} + \frac{z}{3 \text{ mph}} + \frac{y}{6 \text{ mph}} + \frac{x}{4 \text{ mph}} = \frac{x + y + z}{2 \text{ mph}}.$$

That is, $x + y + z = 4$ miles. Thus, she walked $2(x + y + z) = 8$ miles in total. The answer is $\boxed{A}$. □

Problem 18. x and y are positive integers such that $2^8 \cdot 3^2 = x^y$. What is the smallest possible value of $x + y$?

A) 24 B) 48 C) 50 D) 60 E) 128

Solutions for Practice Exam 7

Solution. To minimize $x + y$, we need to find the largest possible y value. Since

$$2^8 \cdot 3^2 = (2^4)^2 \cdot 3^2 = 16^2 \cdot 3^2 = 48^2,$$

we have $x = 48$ and $y = 2$. The answer is $\boxed{C}$. □

Problem 19. How many positive integers smaller than 1000 have exactly 9 positive divisors?

    A) 4   B) 6   C) 8   D) 10   E) None of the preceding

Solution. Let $n < 1000$ be a positive integer having 9 positive divisors. Then, either $n = p^8$ or $n = p^2 q^2$ for some primes p and q with $p < q$. The first case is possible only when $p = 2$. For the latter case, we have $pq < \sqrt{1000} \approx 31.6$. Hence, the possible (p, q) pairs are $(2,3)$, $(2,5)$, $(2,7)$, $(2,11)$, $(2,13)$, $(3,5)$, and $(3,7)$. Thus, there are 8 possible values for n. The answer is $\boxed{C}$. □

Problem 20. As shown in the figure, $\overline{AB}$ is a diameter of a semicircle. C is a point on $\overline{AB}$ with $AC = 4$. D is a point on the arc AB such that $CD = 8$ and $\overline{AB} \perp \overline{CD}$. What is the area of the semicircle?

A) 16π

B) 20π

C) 25π

D) 36π

E) 50π

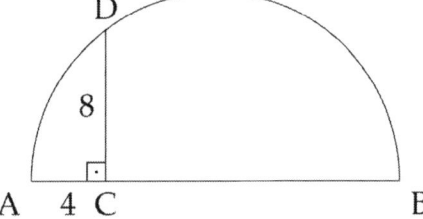

Solution. Let O be the center of the semicircle and r be its radius. Following the figure on the right, we have

$$8^2 + (r - 4)^2 = r^2.$$

That is, $r = 10$. Then the area of the semicircle is

$$\frac{\pi r^2}{2} = 50\pi.$$

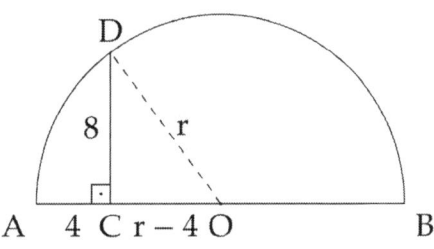

The answer is $\boxed{E}$. □

Problem 21. Let a, b and c be positive integers with $a \leq b$. Suppose $x^a + x^b = x^{111c}$ has a positive integer solution x. Which of the following is always correct?

170

Solutions for Practice Exam 7

A) $a + b = 111c$

B) $111c = a + 1$

C) $x \geq 111c$

D) c is odd number

E) None of the preceding

Solution. We can divide both sides of the equation by x^a to have $1 + x^{b-a} = x^{111c-a}$. That is, $x^{111c-a} - x^{b-a} = 1$, or
$$x^{b-a}(x^{111c-b} - 1) = 1.$$
As x is a positive integer, we have $x^{b-a} = 1$ and $x^{111c-b} = 2$. Then $x = 2$, and therefore $b = a$ and $111c - b = 1$. In other words, $a = b = 111c - 1$. The answer is $\boxed{B}$. □

Problem 22. For some positive integer n, the sum of two real numbers is n, and the sum of their squares is $n + 19$. What is the possible maximum value of n?

A) 5 B) 6 C) 7 D) 8 E) 9

Solution. Suppose x and y are such real numbers: i.e. $x + y = n$ and $x^2 + y^2 = n + 19$. When we substitute $y = n - x$, we have
$$x^2 + (n - x)^2 = n + 19.$$
That is,
$$2x^2 - 2nx + (n^2 - n - 19) = 0.$$
This is a quadratic equation in terms of x, and it has a real number solution when $\Delta \geq 0$. In other words,
$$\Delta = (2n)^2 - 8(n^2 - n - 19) = -4n^2 + 8n + 152 = -4(n-1)^2 + 156 \geq 0.$$
When we solve this inequality, we have $n \leq \sqrt{39} + 1$. Thus, the maximum integer value for n is 7. The answer is $\boxed{C}$. □

Problem 23. Ahmad has 12 marbles. In how many ways can he share with Ben and Cannor so that each of the people has at least 1 marble?

A) 45 B) 55 C) 65 D) 105 E) 132

Solution. Suppose Ahmad gives a of his marbles to Ben and b marbles to Cannor, and he keeps c marbles to himself. Then the number of such ways to share is equal to the number of positive integer solutions to $a + b + c = 12$, which is $C(12-1, 3-1) = C(11, 2) = 55$. The answer is $\boxed{B}$. □

Solutions for Practice Exam 8

Problem 24. What is the area of the right triangle $\triangle ABC$ with side lengths a, b and c, as shown in the figure, satisfying $a + b + c = 28$ and $a^2 + b^2 + c^2 = 288$?

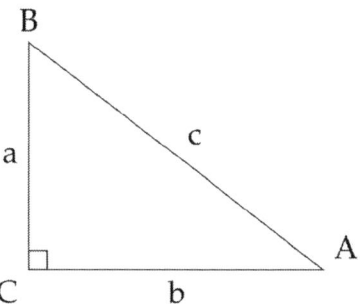

A) 22

B) 24

C) 26

D) 28

E) None of the preceding

Solution. We have $a^2 + b^2 = c^2$ in $\triangle ABC$ by the Pythagorean theorem. Then,
$$288 = a^2 + b^2 + c^2 = 2c^2.$$
That is, $c = 12$. Now, $a + b = 28 - c = 16$ and $a^2 + b^2 = c^2 = 144$. Then,
$$ab = \frac{(a+b)^2 - (a^2+b^2)}{2} = \frac{16^2 - 144}{2} = 56.$$
Thus, the area of $\triangle ABC$ is $\frac{ab}{2} = \frac{56}{2} = 28$. The answer is $\boxed{D}$. □

Problem 25. What is the minimum value of $x+y+z+t$, where x, y, z and t are positive integers satisfying $3^{8x} + 3^{5y} + 3^{12z} = 3^{19t}$?

A) 148 B) 154 C) 160 D) 166 E) 172

Solution. In general, $3^a + 3^b + 3^c = 3^d$ if and only if $a = b = c = d - 1$. Therefore,
$$8x = 5y = 12z = 19t - 1.$$
The least common multiple of 8, 5 and 12 is 120, and the smallest positive integer t such that 120 divides $19t - 1$ is $t = 19$. Hence, $(x, y, z, t) = (45, 72, 30, 19)$, and $x + y + z + t = 166$. The answer is $\boxed{D}$. □

Solutions for Practice Exam 8

Problem 1. If a, b and c are positive integers such that $\frac{a}{b} = 5$ and $\frac{b}{c} = \frac{2}{3}$, then which of the following is the smallest value $a + b + c$ can take?

A) 10 B) 12 C) 14 D) 15 E) 16

Solutions for Practice Exam 8

Solution. Since $\frac{b}{c} = \frac{2}{3}$, we have $b = 2k$ and $c = 3k$ for some positive integer k. However, $\frac{a}{b} = 5$, so $a = 10k$. Then $a + b + c = 15k$. Thus the smallest value of $a + b + c$ is 15 for $k = 1$. The answer is $\boxed{D}$.

Problem 2. On her first day of work, Janabel sold one widget. On day two, she sold three widgets. On day three, she sold five widgets, and on each succeeding day, she sold two more widgets than she had sold on the previous day. How many widgets in total had Janabel sold after working 20 days?

A) 39 B) 99 C) 100 D) 400 E) None of the preceding

Solution. Janabel sold $1 + 3 + 5 + \ldots + 39 = 400$ widgets after 20 days. The answer is $\boxed{D}$.

Problem 3. How many 4-digit positive integers having only odd digits are divisible by 5?

A) 75 B) 80 C) 100 D) 125 E) 150

Solution. As each number is divisible by 5 and contains odd digits, the unit digit is 5. Then, the other digits are $1, 3, 5, 7$ or 9. Thus, there are $5^3 = 125$ such numbers. The answer is $\boxed{D}$.

Problem 4. Two angles of an isosceles triangle measure $80°$ and $x°$. What is the sum of possible values of $x°$?

A) $60°$ B) $70°$ C) $80°$ D) $90°$ E) $150°$

Solution. The possible triangles are 80-80-20 and 50-50-80 triangles. Thus, the sum of the three possible values for x is $20 + 50 + 80 = 150$. The answer is $\boxed{E}$.

Problem 5. If $a + c = 4.98$ and $b + c = 6.48$, what is the value of $b^2 + bc - ab - ca$?

A) 7.47 B) 8.16 C) 9.08 D) 9.72 E) None of the preceding

Solution. Notice that $b^2 + bc - ab - ca = (b - a)(b + c)$. As $b - a = (b + c) - (a + c) = 6.48 - 4.98 = 1.5$, we have $b^2 + bc - ab - ca = (1.5) \cdot (6.48) = 9.72$. The answer is $\boxed{D}$.

Problem 6. What is the tens digit of $15! - 10!$?

A) 0 B) 2 C) 5 D) 8 E) 9

Solutions for Practice Exam 8

Solution. It is enough to compute $15! - 10! \mod 100$. Notice that both $15!$ and $10!$ are divisible by 25 and 4, and therefore by 100. Thus, $15! - 10! \equiv 0 \mod 100$, and so the tens digit is 0. The answer is $\boxed{A}$. □

Problem 7. What is the probability that a randomly chosen 3-digit number between 200 and 300 is divisible by one of its digits?

A) $\dfrac{1}{3}$ B) $\dfrac{23}{33}$ C) $\dfrac{31}{99}$ D) $\dfrac{26}{33}$ E) None of the preceding

Solution. Notice that all of the numbers between 200 and 300 begin with the digit 2. That is, all even numbers (ending in 0, 2, 4, 6, or 8) satisfy the condition as they are divided by 2. Besides, all numbers ending in 1 or 5 satisfy the condition as they are divisible by 1 or 5, respectively. Therefore, the numbers ending in 0, 1, 2, 4, 5, 6, and 8 satisfy the condition, bringing the total number up to 69. For the rest, the numbers ending in 3, 7 or 9 which satisfy the condition are 213, 243, 273, 217, 287, and 279. Thus, the desired probability is $\dfrac{75}{99} = \dfrac{25}{33}$. The answer is $\boxed{E}$. □

Problem 8. What is the area of the region bounded by the x-axis, the y-axis, the line $y = 4x+4$, and the line $y = -x + 9$?

A) 24 B) 32 C) 36 D) 38 E) 40

Solution. Let $A = (x,y)$ be the intersection of the lines $y = 4x + 4$ and $y = -x + 9$. Then,

$$4x + 4 = -x + 9 \implies 5x = 5 \implies x = 1 \implies y = 8.$$

That is, $A = (1,8)$. On the other hand, the y-intercept of the line $y = 4x + 4$ is $B = (0,4)$. Moreover, the x-intercept and y-intercept of the line $y = -x + 9$ are $C = (9,0)$ and $D = (0,9)$. Supposing $O = (0,0)$, we have

$$\begin{aligned}\text{Area}(ABOC) &= \text{Area}(\triangle OCD) - \text{Area}(\triangle ABD) \\ &= \frac{9 \cdot 9}{2} - \frac{5 \cdot 1}{2} \\ &= 38.\end{aligned}$$

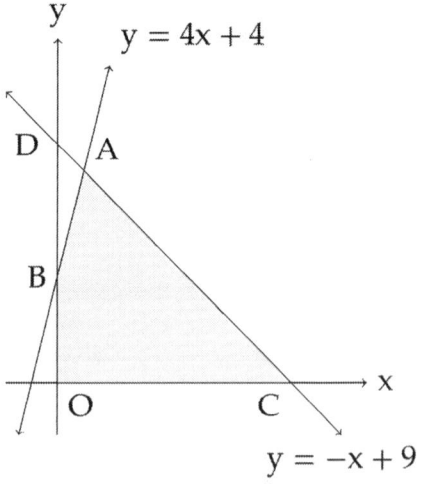

The answer is $\boxed{D}$. □

Problem 9. Suppose a and b represent positive numbers. Of the two numbers, a is the smaller and b the larger. What number represents the point two-thirds of the way between a and b on a

Solutions for Practice Exam 8

number line?

A) $\dfrac{a+b}{3}$ B) $\dfrac{a+2b}{3}$ C) $\dfrac{3a+b}{3}$ D) $\dfrac{2a+2b}{3}$ E) None of the preceding

Solution. As $b > a$, the distance between them is $b - a$. Thus, the number representing two-thirds of the distance from a to b is $a + \dfrac{2(b-a)}{3} = \dfrac{a+2b}{3}$. The answer is $\boxed{B}$. □

Problem 10. How many positive integer values for n make $n^{18/n}$ an integer?

A) 5   B) 6   C) 7   D) 8   E) None of the preceding

Solution. The positive values for n which make $n^{18/n}$ an integer are 1, 2, 3, 4, 6, 9, 18, 27 and 36. Thus, there are 9 integer values for n. The answer is $\boxed{E}$. □

Problem 11. A circle is inscribed in a square of side length of 4. A point X is randomly and uniformly chosen inside the square. What is the probability that X is inside the circle?

A) $\dfrac{\pi}{6}$ B) $\dfrac{\pi}{4}$ C) $\dfrac{2\pi}{3}$ D) $\dfrac{3\pi}{4}$ E) $\dfrac{5\pi}{6}$

Solution. The area of the circle is 4π, and the area of the square is 16, making the probability $4\pi/16 = \pi/4$. The answer is $\boxed{B}$. □

Problem 12. $\triangle ABC$ is an isosceles triangle with $AB = AC$. Point D is on $\overline{BC}$ such that $3m\angle CAD = m\angle BAD$. If $m\angle ADC = 110°$, what is the $m\angle ABC$?

A) 30°
B) 35°
C) 40°
D) 45°
E) 50°

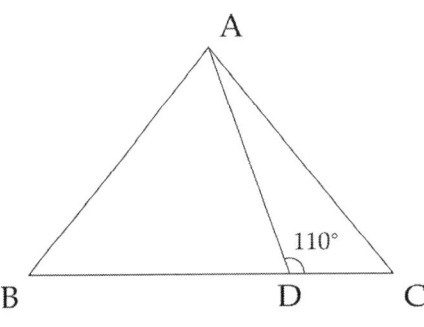

Solutions for Practice Exam 8

Solution. Let $m\angle CAD = \alpha$ and $m\angle ABC = \beta$. Then, $m\angle BAD = 3\alpha$ and $m\angle ACD = \beta$. Also, $\alpha + \beta = 70°$ and $3\alpha + \beta = 110°$. Therefore, $\alpha = 20°$ and $\beta = 50°$. The answer is $\boxed{E}$. □

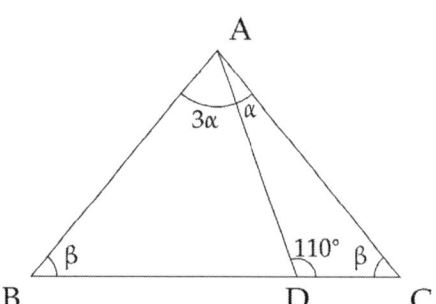

Problem 13. Josh bought 4 lb. of apples, 5 lb. of bananas, and 3 lb. of peaches for $7. Sam bought 2 lb. of apples, 1 lb. of bananas, and 3 lb. of peaches for $5 from the same store. If somebody wants to buy 1 lb. of bananas, 1 lb. of apples, and 1 lb. of peaches, then how much will the total cost be?

A) $3.5 B) $3 C) $2 D) $1.5 E) $1

Solution. Suppose 1 lb of apples is $A, 1 lb of bananas is $B, and 1 lb of peaches is $P. Then $4A + 5B + 3P = 7$ and $2A + B + 3P = 5$. Hence,

$$A + B + P = \frac{(4A + 5B + 3P) + (2A + B + 3P)}{6} = \frac{7 + 5}{6} = 2.$$

The answer is $\boxed{C}$. □

Problem 14. Both roots of the quadratic equation $x^2 - 19x + k$ are prime numbers. What is the number of possible values of k?

A) 0 B) 1 C) 2 D) 5 E) Infinitely many

Solution. Let p and q be prime numbers so that they are the roots of $x^2 - 19x + k$. Then $p + q = 19$ and $pq = k$. Such a tuple of prime numbers can only be $(2, 17)$. Thus, there is only one possible value for k. The answer is $\boxed{B}$. □

Problem 15. A jar contains 3 red and 4 green balls. Two balls are drawn at random without replacement. If the two balls have different colors, what is the probability that the second ball is green?

A) $\frac{1}{2}$ B) $\frac{1}{3}$ C) $\frac{1}{4}$ D) $\frac{1}{5}$ E) None of the preceding

Solutions for Practice Exam 8

Solution. Let X be the case that the two balls have different colors, and Y be the case that the second ball is green. We are asked to compute Pr(Y|X), that is,

$$\Pr(Y|X) = \frac{\Pr(X \cap Y)}{\Pr(X)}.$$

Since $\Pr(X) = \frac{3}{7} \cdot \frac{4}{6} + \frac{4}{7} \cdot \frac{3}{6} = \frac{4}{7}$ and $\Pr(X \cap Y) = \frac{3}{7} \cdot \frac{4}{6} = \frac{2}{7}$, we have $\Pr(Y|X) = \frac{2/7}{4/7} = \frac{1}{2}$. The answer is $\boxed{A}$. □

Problem 16. Suppose ABCD is a square with side length 2 units. If a circle tangent to $\overline{AB}$ at E contains C and D, what is the radius of the circle?

A) 1

B) $\frac{5}{4}$

C) $\frac{5}{2}$

D) $\frac{6}{5}$

E) None of the preceding

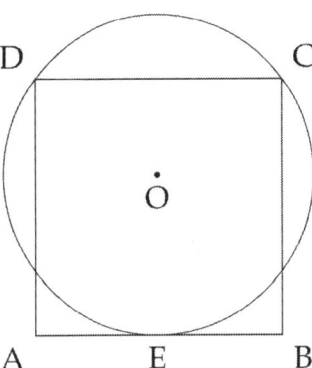

Solution. Let F and G be the points where the circle intersects $\overline{AD}$ and $\overline{BC}$ respectively. As AE = BE = 1, we have

$$AE^2 = AF \cdot AD \implies 1 = AF \cdot 2 \implies AF = \frac{1}{2},$$

$$BE^2 = BG \cdot BC \implies 1 = BG \cdot 2 \implies BG = \frac{1}{2}.$$

Thus, the radius of the circle is $\frac{1}{2} + \frac{2 - 1/2}{2} = \frac{5}{4}$. The answer is $\boxed{B}$. □

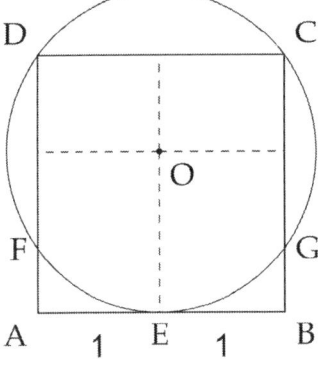

Problem 17. Two different integers a and b satisfy the equation $5^a + 7^b = 6(7b - 5a)$. What is the value of a + b?

A) 0 B) 1 C) 2 D) 3 E) 4

Solution. Notice that a and b are nonnegative integers, otherwise, the left hand side of the equation is not an integer while the right hand side is. Also

$$5^a + 7^b = 6(7b - 5a) \implies (5^a + 30a) + (7^b - 42b) = 0.$$

Solutions for Practice Exam 8

Since $5^a + 30a > 0$, we should have $7^b - 42b < 0$. However, 7^b is an exponential function and $42b$ is a linear function, in terms of b. That is, 7^b grows faster than $42b$. Hence, we conclude that $7^b < 42b$ only when $b = 1$ or $b = 2$. In both cases, we obtain $a = 1$. Since a and b are different, we only have the solution $(1, 2)$, that is, $a + b = 3$. The answer is $\boxed{D}$. □

Problem 18. Let a, b and c be distinct prime numbers such that $a(c-b) = 18$ and $b(c-a) = 40$. What is the value of $a + b + c$?

A) 13 B) 17 C) 19 D) 21 E) None of the preceding

Solution. From the given equations, a is either 2 or 3, and b is either 2 or 5. Since all are distinct, (a, b) is either $(2, 5)$, $(3, 2)$ or $(3, 5)$. If $(a, b) = (2, 5)$, the first equation gives $c = 14$, which is not possible. If $(a, b) = (3, 2)$, the first equation gives $c = 8$, which is again not possible. If $(a, b) = (3, 5)$, both the first equation and the second equation give $c = 11$. Thus, $a + b + c = 3 + 5 + 11 = 19$. The answer is $\boxed{C}$. □

Problem 19. How many pairs of positive integers (m, n) satisfy $n + m^2 \leq 29$?

A) 30 B) 43 C) 59 D) 85 E) 90

Solution. Notice that $m \leq 5$. Then, for each $m = 1, 2, 3, 4, 5$, we have $n \leq 29 - m^2$. That is, there are $29 - m^2$ pairs (m, n) for each m. Thus, there are

$$\sum_{m=1}^{5} (29 - m^2) = 28 + 25 + 20 + 13 + 4 = 90$$

pairs in total. The answer is $\boxed{E}$. □

Problem 20. Suppose ABCD is a square with $AB = 30$. If K is the intersection of its diagonals, and L is on $\overline{AB}$ such that $AL = 7$, what is the value of KL?

A) 13
B) 15
C) 17
D) $15\sqrt{2}$
E) None of the preceding

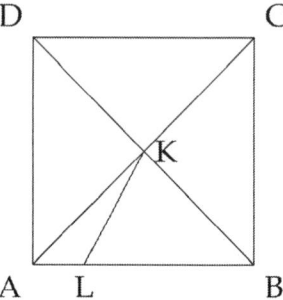

Solutions for Practice Exam 8

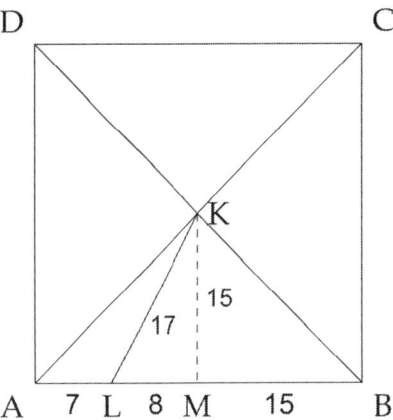

Solution. Pick a point M on $\overline{AB}$ such that $\overline{KM} \perp \overline{AB}$. Then $AM = MB = KM = 15$ since K is the intersection of diagonals. As $AL = 7$, we have $LM = 8$. Thus, $KL = \sqrt{15^2 + 8^2} = 17$. The answer is $\boxed{C}$. □

Problem 21. Suppose A, B, and C represent digits different than zero such that the sum AAA+BBB+CCC of three-digit numbers equals the four-digit number ABBC. Find the value of A+B+C.

A) 14   B) 16   C) 18   D) 23   E) 24

Solution. $AAA + BBB + CCC = ABBC \implies 111A + 111B + 111C = 1000A + 110B + C \implies 110C + B = 889A$. There is only one solution (A, B, C) over digits, and it is $(1, 9, 8)$. Thus, $A + B + C = 18$. The answer is $\boxed{C}$. □

Problem 22. As n ranges over all positive integers, how many distinct values can be found for the greatest common divisor of $6n + 15$ and $10n + 21$?

A) 2   B) 3   C) 4   D) 5   E) 6

Solution. We have

$$\gcd(6n + 15, 10n + 21) = \gcd(6n + 15, 10n + 21 - (6n + 15)) = \gcd(6n + 15, 4n + 6)$$
$$= \gcd(6n + 15 - (4n + 6), 4n + 6) = \gcd(2n + 9, 4n + 6)$$
$$= \gcd(2n + 9, 4n + 6 - 2(2n + 9)) = \gcd(2n + 9, -12)$$

Then $\gcd(6n + 15, 10n + 21)$ divides 12. Besides, it cannot be an even number because $2n + 9$ is an odd number. Thus, the possible values for $\gcd(6n + 15, 10n + 21)$ are 1 and 3. Actually, it is 1 when $n = 1$, and 3 when $n = 3$. The answer is $\boxed{A}$.

Alternative Solution. Notice that $5(6n + 15) - 3(10n + 21) = 12$. Therefore, the greatest common divisor of $6n + 15$ and $10n + 21$ divides 12. However, it cannot be even because both $6n + 15$ and $10n + 21$ are odd. Thus, the greatest common divisor of $6n + 15$ and $10n + 21$ is either 1 or 3. Actually, it is 1 when $n = 1$, and 3 when $n = 3$. The answer is $\boxed{A}$. □

Solutions for Practice Exam 8

Problem 23. How many ordered pairs of integers (a, b) satisfy the equation $a^4 + b^2 = 4b$?

A) 2 B) 4 C) 5 D) 6 E) 8

Solution. Notice that

$$a^4 + b^2 = 4b \implies (b-2)^2 = b^2 - 4b + 4 = -a^4 + 4.$$

Therefore, $-a^4 + 4 \geq 0$. This is only possible when $a = 0$ or $a = \pm 1$. However, b is also an integer. Therefore, the only (a, b) solutions are $(0, 0)$ and $(0, 4)$. The answer is $\boxed{A}$. □

Problem 24. Let P be a point inside of equilateral triangle $\triangle ABC$ such that $m\angle APB = 150°$, $AP = 2\sqrt{3}$ and $BP = 2$. What is the value of PC?

A) 2 B) $2\sqrt{3}$ C) 4 D) $4\sqrt{3}$ E) 6

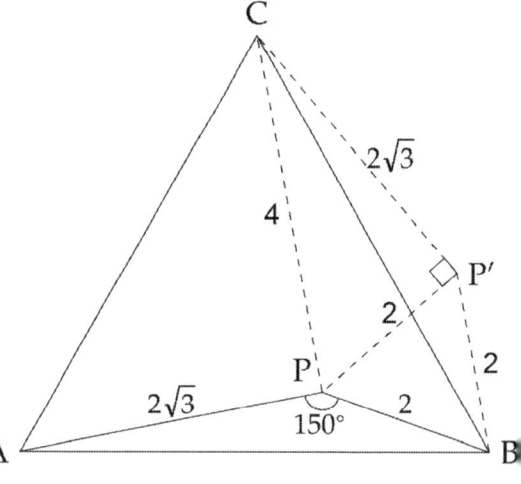

Solution. When we copy $\triangle APB$ onto $\overline{BC}$ as $\triangle CP'B$, we have

$$PB = P'B = 2 \text{ and } m\angle PBP' = 60°.$$

Then, $\triangle PBP'$ is an equilateral triangle. As $m\angle BP'C = 150°$, we have

$$m\angle PP'C = 150° - 60° = 90°.$$

Then $PC = \sqrt{(2\sqrt{3})^2 + 2^2} = 4$. The answer is $\boxed{C}$. □

Problem 25. Suppose $n > 1$ is an integer. For each $k = 1, 2, \ldots, n$, let $d(k)$ be the number of digits in k (e.g., $d(32) = 2, d(708) = 3, d(60093) = 5$, and so on). If

$$d(1) + d(2) + \cdots + d(n) = 2013,$$

find the digit sum of n (e.g., the digit sum of 65003 is $6 + 5 + 0 + 0 + 3 = 14$).

A) 5 B) 14 C) 15 D) 16 E) 19

Solutions for Practice Exam 9

Solution. We have $d(k) = 1$ for $k = 1, \ldots, 9$, $d(k) = 2$ for $k = 10, \ldots, 99$, and $d(k) = 3$ for $k = 100, \ldots, 999$. Assuming that n is a three-digit number, we have

$$2013 = \sum_{k=1}^{n} d(k) = \sum_{k=1}^{9} d(k) + \sum_{k=10}^{99} d(k) + \sum_{k=100}^{n} d(k)$$

$$= \sum_{k=1}^{9} 1 + \sum_{k=10}^{99} 2 + \sum_{k=100}^{n} 3$$

$$= 9 + 180 + 3(n - 100 + 1) = 3n - 108.$$

Thus, $n = 707$, and therefore the digit sum of n is $7 + 0 + 7 = 14$. The answer is $\boxed{B}$. $\square$

Solutions for Practice Exam 9

Problem 1. Suppose $x + \dfrac{1}{y} = 3.125$. Find the decimal equal to $\dfrac{y}{xy+1}$.

A) 0.25 B) 0.32 C) 0.8 D) 1.25 E) 3.35

Solution. $x + \dfrac{1}{y} = 3.125 \implies \dfrac{xy+1}{y} = 3.125 \implies \dfrac{y}{xy+1} = \dfrac{1}{3.125} = 0.32$. The answer is $\boxed{B}$. $\square$

Problem 2. A four-digit number $53xy$ is divisible by 3, 4, and 5. What is the sum of all possible x values?

A) 4 B) 7 C) 11 D) 12 E) 13

Solution. As $53xy$ is divisible by 5 and 4, $y = 0$ and x is either 0, 2, 4, 6 or 8. As $53xy$ is also divisible by 3, $5 + 3 + x + y = 8 + x$ is divisible by 3. This is possible only when $x = 4$. The answer is $\boxed{A}$. $\square$

Problem 3. A mathematical game on a computer changes the number displayed on the screen when you press A, B, or C. It adds 3 when you click on A, subtracts 3 when you click on B, and divides by 2 when you click on C. If the number currently displayed is 64, what is the least number of clicks required to get the number 1?

A) 4 B) 5 C) 6 D) 7 E) 8

Solution. By pressing C four times, we have

$$64 \div 2 = 32, \rightarrow 32 \div 2 = 16, \rightarrow 16 \div 2 = 8 \rightarrow 8 \div 2 = 4.$$

Then we press B to get $4 - 3 = 1$. In total, we press five times. The answer is $\boxed{B}$. $\square$

Solutions for Practice Exam 9

Problem 4. The lengths, in inches, of the sides of the equilateral triangle are $a + 2b$, $3a - b$, and $5b - a$. Which of the following **could not** be the values of a and b?

A) $(12, 8)$ B) $\left(\dfrac{9}{2}, 3\right)$ C) $(10, 6)$ D) $(3, 2)$ E) $\left(\dfrac{3}{2}, 1\right)$

Solution. For each (a, b) given in the choices, we can check whether the triangle is equilateral:

$(a, b) = (12, 8) \implies$ the side lengths are $28, 28, 28 \implies$ it is a equilateral triangle.

$(a, b) = (9/2, 3) \implies$ the side lengths are $21/2, 21/2, 21/2 \implies$ it is a equilateral triangle.

$(a, b) = (10, 6) \implies$ the side lengths are $22, 24, 20 \implies$ it is NOT a equilateral triangle.

$(a, b) = (3, 2) \implies$ the side lengths are $7, 7, 7 \implies$ it is a equilateral triangle.

$(a, b) = (3/2, 1) \implies$ the side lengths are $7/2, 7/2, 7/2 \implies$ it is a equilateral triangle.

Therefore, the answer is $\boxed{C}$. □

Problem 5. When an empty jar is filled with water, it weighs 6 pounds. When 3/7 of the water is poured out, the jar weighs 4 pounds. How much does the empty jar weigh in pounds?

A) $\dfrac{4}{3}$ B) $\dfrac{3}{2}$ C) $\dfrac{5}{3}$ D) 2 E) $\dfrac{5}{2}$

Solution. Let X be the weight of the empty jar and Y be the weight of the water when the jar is full of water. Then

$$X + Y = 6 \text{ pounds} \quad \text{and} \quad X + \frac{4Y}{7} = 4 \text{ pounds}.$$

Thus, $X = \dfrac{4}{3}$ pounds and $Y = \dfrac{14}{3}$ pounds. The answer is $\boxed{A}$. □

Problem 6. What is the largest value for the length of a list of consecutive integers whose sum is 55?

A) 10   B) 25   C) 55   D) 110   E) 135

Solution. Let $n, n+1, \ldots, n+(k-1)$ be such consecutive integers. Then

$$55 = n + (n+1) + \ldots + (n+(k-1)) = kn + \frac{(k-1)k}{2} = \frac{k(2n+k-1)}{2}.$$

That is, $110 = k(2n + k - 1)$. Thus, k divides 110. To make k be the largest value, we have $n = -54$ and $k = 110$. In fact, the sum of the numbers $-54, -53, \ldots, 54, 55$ is 55. Thus, the answer is $\boxed{D}$. □

Solutions for Practice Exam 9

Problem 7. You have six sticks of the following lengths: 1 cm, 2 cm, 3 cm, 11 cm, 12 cm, and 13 cm. You have to choose three of these sticks to form a triangle. How many different choices of three sticks are there that work?

A) 4 B) 5 C) 6 D) 7 E) 8

Solution. We check whether the triangle inequality is satisfied or not. Clearly, we cannot choose the stick of length 1 cm because the triangle inequality is not satisfy whatever the other sticks are. In that sense, there are $C(5,3) = 10$ ways to pick three sticks:

$$
\begin{array}{llll}
(2, 3, 11) & \to \text{No,} & (2, 12, 13) & \to \text{Yes} \\
(2, 3, 12) & \to \text{No,} & (3, 11, 12) & \to \text{Yes} \\
(2, 3, 13) & \to \text{No,} & (3, 11, 12) & \to \text{Yes} \\
(2, 11, 12) & \to \text{Yes,} & (3, 12, 13) & \to \text{Yes} \\
(2, 11, 13) & \to \text{No,} & (11, 12, 13) & \to \text{Yes}
\end{array}
$$

Therefore, there are 6 ways to construct a triangle. The answer is $\boxed{C}$.

Problem 8. Two lines which intersect at $(2,2)$ have slopes -2 and $\frac{1}{2}$. What is the area of the triangle enclosed by these two lines and the line $x = 0$?

A) 4 B) 8 C) 10 D) 12 E) None of the preceding

Solution. The equations of the lines are

$$y - 2 = -2(x - 2) \implies y = -2x + 6$$

and

$$y - 2 = \frac{1}{2}(x - 2) \implies y = \frac{1}{2}x + 1.$$

Those lines intersect at $(0, 6)$ and $(0, 1)$ with the line $x = 0$. Then, the area of the triangle is

$$\frac{(6 - 1) \cdot 2}{2} = 5.$$

The answer is $\boxed{E}$.

Problem 9. In the table the sum of the entries in each column, row, and diagonal is equal to 42. What is the value of c?

Solutions for Practice Exam 9

A) 6
B) 8
C) 10
D) 12
E) 14

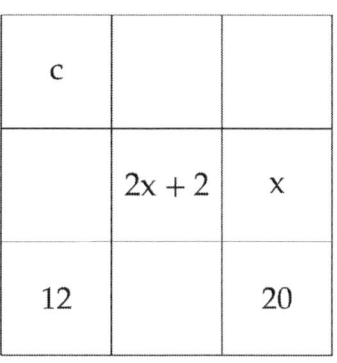

Solution. Considering the sums in the 3rd row, 2nd row, 2nd column and 3rd column, we fill the blanks in the figure. Then, considering the 1st row and 1st column, we have $c = 3x - 10$. Now, considering the diagonal (upper left to lower right), we have

$$42 = (3x - 10) + (2x + 2) + 20 = 5x + 12.$$

That is, $x = 6$. Thus, $c = 8$. The answer is $\boxed{B}$. □

Problem 10. Which of the following is equal to the sum of primes p such that $p^2 + 11$ has exactly 9 positive divisors? (Include 1 and the number itself.)

A) 2 B) 3 C) 5 D) 7 E) More than 7

Solution. Notice that $p^2 + 11$ has exactly 9 positive divisors if and only if $p^2 + 11 = q^8$ or $p^2 + 11 = q^2 \cdot r^2$ for some primes q and r with $q < r$. Also notice that $p \neq 2$, because $2^2 + 11 = 15 = 3 \cdot 5$ has 4 positive divisors. Hence, p is an odd prime, and therefore, $p^2 + 11$ is divisible by 4 because $p^2 \equiv 1 \mod 4$. However, $p^2 + 11 = q^8$ is divisible by 4 only if $q = 2$. In this case, $p^2 = 245$, which is not possible. On the other hand, $p^2 + 11 = q^2 \cdot r^2$ is divisible by 4 only if $q = 2$. In this case, $p^2 + 11 = 4r^2 \implies 4r^2 - p^2 = 11 \implies (2r - p)(2r + p) = 11$. This is possible only when $2r - p = 1$ and $2r + p = 11$, that is, when $r = 3$ and $p = 5$. Hence, there is only one such prime p, which is 5. The answer is $\boxed{C}$. □

Problem 11. How many three digit numbers have digits whose product is 12?

A) 3 B) 6 C) 9 D) 12 E) 15

Solution. It is enough to choose 3 nonzero digits such that their product is $12 = 2 \times 2 \times 3$, where the order matters. There are 3 ways to distribute the 3, and there are 6 ways to distribute the 2's. Therefore, there are $3 \times 6 = 18$ total combinations. However, as it is noticed that the only non-digit factor of 12 is 12, the 3 combinations 1 1 12, 1 12 1, and 12 1 1 do not make 3 digit

Solutions for Practice Exam 9

numbers. Thus, there are $18 - 3 = 15$ three-digit numbers whose product is 12. The answer is $\boxed{E}$. □

Problem 12. The two legs of a right triangle, which are altitudes, have lengths $4\sqrt{3}$ and 12. How long is the third altitude of the triangle?

A) 2 B) 4 C) 5 D) 6 E) 8

Solution. Let the third altitude of the triangle be of length x. Since the length of the third side is $\sqrt{(4\sqrt{3})^2 + 12^2} = 8\sqrt{3}$, and the area of the triangle is $\frac{4\sqrt{3} \cdot 12}{2} = 24\sqrt{3}$, we have $24\sqrt{3} = \frac{x \cdot 8\sqrt{3}}{2}$. Hence $x = 6$. The answer is $\boxed{D}$. □

Problem 13. Based on the pattern, find how many more shaded squares than unshaded squares will be in the 50th diagram in the sequence.

A) 50
B) 60
C) 80
D) 100
E) 150

Solution. Let N_k be the number of shaded squares in the k-th diagram. Notice that $N_1 = 0$, $N_2 = N_3 = 3$, $N_4 = N_5 = 3 + 7 = 10$. As it goes on, we have

$$N_{2k} = N_{2k+1} = 3 + 7 + \ldots + (4k - 1).$$

Then,

$$N_{50} = 3 + 7 + \ldots + 99 = \sum_{n=1}^{25}(4n-1) = \left(4\sum_{n=1}^{25} n\right) - 25 = \frac{4(25)(26)}{2} - 25 = 1275.$$

However, there are $50^2 = 2500$ squares in total, therefore, there are $2500 - 1275 = 1225$ unshaded squares. Thus, their difference is $1275 - 1225 = 50$. The answer is $\boxed{A}$. □

Problem 14. Suppose abcd and badc are four-digit numbers. If $abcd - badc = 1818$, then find $(a - b) + (d - c)$.

A) 0 B) 2 C) 4 D) 6 E) None of the preceding

Solution. $1818 = abcd - badc = 900a - 900b + 9c - 9d = 900(a-b) + 9(c-d)$. Thus, $a - b = 2$ and $c - d = 2$. Then $(a - b) + (d - c) = 2 - 2 = 0$. The answer is $\boxed{A}$. □

185

Solutions for Practice Exam 9

Problem 15. A triple (x, y, z) of integers with $x, y, z \geq 0$ is chosen at random such that $2x + y + z = 4$. What is the probability that $x + y + z = 3$?

A) $\dfrac{4}{9}$ B) $\dfrac{5}{9}$ C) $\dfrac{11}{18}$ D) $\dfrac{2}{3}$ E) None of the preceding

Solution. The solutions satisfying $2x + y + z = 4$ are $(0, 0, 4)$, $(0, 1, 3)$, $(0, 2, 2)$, $(0, 3, 1)$, $(0, 4, 0)$, $(1, 0, 2)$, $(1, 1, 1)$, $(1, 2, 0)$, $(2, 0, 0)$. Thus, there are 9 solutions. On the other hand, $x + y + z = 3$ if and only if $x = 1$, because $x = (2x + y + z) - (x + y + z) = 4 - 3 = 1$ in that case. There are three solutions where $x = 1$. The answer is $\boxed{E}$.   □

Problem 16. $\triangle ABC$ is a triangle with $AC = 12$. The bisector of $\angle A$ meets $\overline{BC}$ at D, and $CD = 4$. The set of all possible values of AB is an open interval (a, b). What is $a + b$?

A) 20   B) 24   C) 28   D) 30   E) 32

Solution. As $\overline{AD}$ is the bisector of $\angle A$, we have
$$\frac{AB}{BD} = \frac{AC}{CD} = \frac{12}{4} = 3.$$

By supposing $BD = k$, we have $AB = 3k$. Using the triangle inequality, we have

$$3k + (k + 4) > 12 \quad \text{and} \quad 12 + (k + 4) > 3k.$$

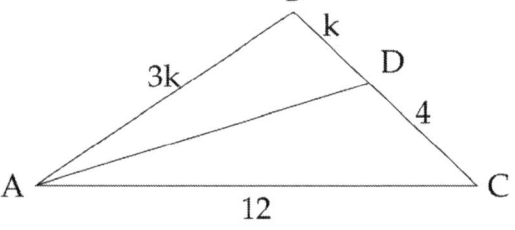

That is, $2 < k < 8$. Then $6 < AB = 3k < 24$, and therefore, $a + b = 6 + 24 = 30$. The answer is $\boxed{D}$.   □

Problem 17. Suppose $a, b,$ and c are positive integers such that $a + \dfrac{1}{b + \dfrac{1}{c+1}} = \dfrac{23}{7}$. Find $2a + b + c$.

A) 7   B) 8   C) 9   D) 10   E) None of the preceding

Solution. Notice that
$$\frac{23}{7} = 3 + \frac{2}{7} = 3 + \frac{1}{\frac{7}{2}} = 3 + \frac{1}{3 + \frac{1}{2}}.$$

Thus, $a = 3$, $b = 3$ and $c = 1$. Then, $2a + b + c = 10$. The answer is $\boxed{D}$.   □

Solutions for Practice Exam 9

Problem 18. How many integer pairs (m, n) satisfy the equation $m \cdot n + n + 14 = (m-1)^2$?

A) 2 B) 6 C) 8 D) 10 E) 12

Solution. Using the given equation, we have

$$m \cdot n + n + 14 = (m-1)^2 \implies n = \frac{m^2 - 2m - 13}{m+1} = (m-3) - \frac{10}{m+1}.$$

As n is an integer, $m + 1$ divides 10. That is, $m + 1$ is either $\pm 1, \pm 2, \pm 5$ or ± 10. Since each of those values gives an (m, n) pair, there are 8 solutions. The answer is $\boxed{C}$.

Problem 19. How many four-digit positive integers can be found so that all four digits are prime numbers and the sum of the digits is even?

A) 172 B) 168 C) 150 D) 144 E) 136

Solution. The prime digits are 2, 3, 5 and 7. The sum of digits is even when 2 is used an even number times. If 2 is never used, there are $3^4 = 81$ such numbers. If 2 is used twice, there are $C(4, 2) \cdot 3^2 = 54$ such numbers. If 2 is used four times, the number is 2222. Thus, there are $81 + 54 + 1 = 136$ such numbers. The answer is $\boxed{E}$.

Problem 20. ABCD is a trapezoid with $\overline{AD} \parallel \overline{BC}$, $\overline{AB} \perp \overline{AD}$, $AB = 8$, $AD = 6$ and $DC = EC = 10$. What is the area of ABDE?

A) 28
B) 32
C) 36
D) 40
E) None of the preceding

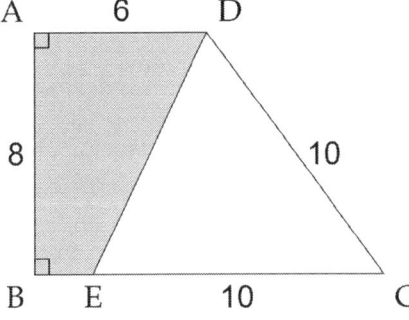

Solution. Let F be a point on $\overline{BC}$ such that $\overline{DF} \perp \overline{BC}$. Then, BFDA is a rectangle with side lengths 6 and 8. As $\triangle DFC$ is a right triangle, we have $FC = 6$. Then, $EF = 4$ and $BE = 2$. Thus, the area of ABDE is

$$\frac{(6+2) \cdot 8}{2} = 32.$$

The answer is $\boxed{B}$.

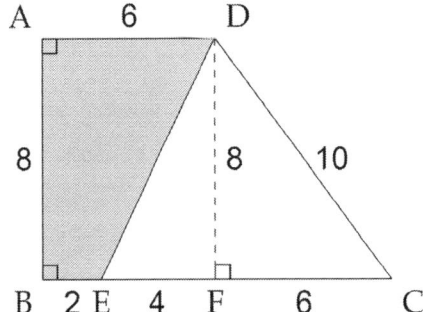

Solutions for Practice Exam 9

Problem 21. The real number $\sqrt{19 - 8\sqrt{3}}$ can be expressed in the form $a + b\sqrt{3}$ where a and b are integers and a is positive. What is the value of $a + b$?

A) 3   B) 4   C) 6   D) 7   E) 8

Solution. Notice that $\sqrt{19 - 8\sqrt{3}} = \sqrt{19 - 2\sqrt{48}} = \sqrt{(\sqrt{16} - \sqrt{3})^2} = \sqrt{16} - \sqrt{3} = 4 - \sqrt{3}$. Thus, $a = 4$ and $b = -1$. Then, $a + b = 4 - 1 = 3$. The answer is $\boxed{A}$. □

Problem 22. An EZ number is defined as any positive integer with the following properties: i) It has at least two digits, ii) All its digits are the same, and iii) It has exactly 4 positive divisors. For example, $111 = 3 \times 37$ is an EZ number. How many EZ numbers less than 10^5 are there?

A) 7   B) 17   C) 27   D) 37   E) None of the preceding

Solution. The numbers less than 10^5 are of at most 5 digits. A two-digit number aa is an EZ number if and only if a is prime number, because $aa = 11 \cdot a$ has 4 divisors only when a is a prime digit. A three digit number aaa is an EZ number only when $a = 1$, because $aaa = 111 \cdot a = 3 \cdot 37 \cdot a$ has 4 divisors only when $a = 1$. A four digit number aaaa is an EZ number only when $a = 1$, because $aaaa = 1111 \cdot a = 11 \cdot 101 \cdot a$ has 4 divisors only when $a = 1$. A five digit number aaaaa is an EZ number only when $a = 1$, because $aaaaa = 11111 \cdot a = 41 \cdot 271 \cdot a$ has 4 divisors only when $a = 1$. Thus, the EZ numbers less than 10^5 are

$$22, 33, 55, 77, 111, 1111, 11111.$$

The answer is $\boxed{A}$. □

Problem 23. In a local soccer league with 5 teams, one team plays a total of 20 games. For example, Team A plays with the other 4 teams a total of five times. For each team the below table shows the number of W (Win)- L (Lost)- T- (Tie). What is $x + y - z$?

A) 12
B) 13
C) 14
D) 15
E) None of the preceding

Team	W	L	T
A	2	15	3
B	7	9	4
C	6	12	2
D	10	8	2
E	x	y	z

Solution. As each team plays 20 games, $x + y + z = 20$. On the other hand, for each game, one team wins and so the other team loses, unless the game finishes in a tie. In that sense,

Solutions for Practice Exam 9

there are two possible outcomes: either one W and one L, or, two T's. Therefore, the sum of W's and the sum of L's are equal:

$$2 + 7 + 6 + 10 + x = 15 + 9 + 12 + 8 + y,$$

and the sum of T's are even:

$$3 + 4 + 2 + 2 + z \text{ is even.}$$

That is, $x = y + 19$ and z is odd. Since x, y, z are non-negative numbers, the only possible solution is $(x, y, z) = (19, 0, 1)$. Thus, $x + y - z = 19 + 0 - 1 = 18$. The answer is $\boxed{E}$. □

Problem 24. Suppose ABCD is a trapezoid such that AB ∥ CD, AD = 8, DC = 11, BC = 15, and m∠C + m∠D = 270°. What is the value of AB?

A) 26
B) 28
C) 30
D) 32
E) 34

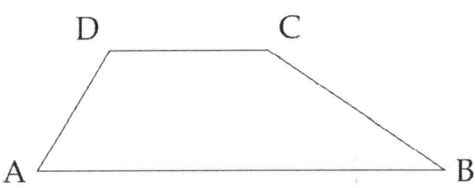

Solution. Let E be the intersection point of $\overleftrightarrow{AD}$ and $\overleftrightarrow{BC}$. Suppose DE = x and CE = y. Then, using the similarity between △EDC and △EAB, we have

$$\frac{x}{x+8} = \frac{y}{y+15} = \frac{11}{AB}.$$

That is, $y = \frac{15x}{8}$. On the other hand, since m∠C + m∠D = 270°, we have m∠E = 90°. Thus, $x^2 + y^2 = 11^2$ in △EDC, we get $x = \frac{88}{17}$. Thus,

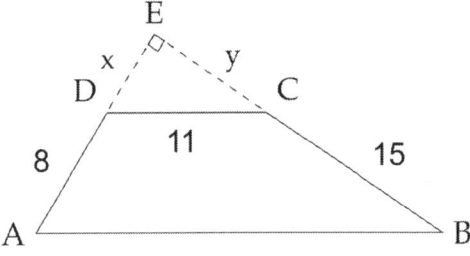

$$AB = 11 \cdot \frac{x+8}{x} = 28.$$

The answer is $\boxed{B}$. □

Problem 25. Suppose n is a positive integer. If 2019 digits are used to enumerate the positive integers less than n, what is the digit sum of n?

A) 610   B) 660   C) 710   D) 760   E) None of the preceding

Solutions for Practice Exam 10

Solution. The number of digits used in one-digit numbers is 9. The number of digits used in two-digit numbers is $2 \cdot 90 = 180$. Thus, there are $2019 - (9 + 180) = 1830$ digits to use in three-digit numbers. So, $1830/3 = 610$ three-digit numbers. Then, $n = 99 + 610 + 1 = 710$. The answer is $\boxed{C}$. □

Solutions for Practice Exam 10

Problem 1. What is 20% of $5^{32} - 5^{30}$?

A) $6 \cdot 5^{28}$ B) $8 \cdot 5^{30}$ C) $24 \cdot 5^{29}$ D) $12 \cdot 5^{29}$ E) $24 \cdot 5^{28}$

Solution. As $20\% = \dfrac{20}{100} = \dfrac{1}{5}$, we have that 20% of $(5^{32} - 5^{30})$ is

$$\frac{1}{5} \cdot (5^{32} - 5^{30}) = \frac{1}{5} \cdot 5^{30} \cdot (5^2 - 1) = 5^{29} \cdot 24.$$

The answer is $\boxed{C}$. □

Problem 2. If $N = 2018^2 + 4 \cdot 2018 + 4$, then what is the sum of the distinct prime factors of N?

A) 14 B) 17 C) 108 D) 2017 E) 2011

Solution.
$$N = 2018^2 + 4 \cdot 2018 + 4 = (2018 + 2)^2 = 2020^2 = 2^4 \cdot 5^2 \cdot 101^2.$$
Thus, the sum of the prime factors of n is $2 + 5 + 101 = 108$. The answer is $\boxed{C}$. □

Problem 3. In a mathematics contest with ten problems, a student gains 5 points for a correct answer and loses 2 points for an incorrect answer. If Olivia answered every problem and her score was 29, how many correct answers did she have?

A) 3 B) 4 C) 5 D) 6 E) 7

Solution. Suppose Olivia solved a problems correctly. Then, the number of incorrect answers is $10 - a$, and therefore $29 = 5 \cdot a - 2 \cdot (10 - a) = 7a - 20$. Thus, $a = 7$. The answer is $\boxed{E}$. □

Problem 4. A square has side length x. To make a new square, the side lengths are increased by 1. The difference between the areas of two squares is 101. What is the value of x?

A) 31 B) 40 C) 45 D) 49 E) 50

Solution. $101 = (x + 1)^2 - x^2 = 2x + 1$. Thus, $x = 50$. The answer is $\boxed{E}$. □

Solutions for Practice Exam 10

Problem 5. Find the value of x for which $100^x \cdot 1000^{2x} = 10000^{10}$.

A) 3 B) 4 C) 5 D) 6 E) 7

Solution. Notice that $100 = 10^2$, $1000 = 10^3$ and $10000 = 10^4$. Therefore,

$$(10^2)^x \cdot (10^3)^{2x} = (10^4)^{10} \Rightarrow 10^{8x} = 10^{40} \Rightarrow x = 5.$$

The answer is $\boxed{C}$.

Problem 6. If $1! \cdot 2! \cdot 3! \cdots 10! \cdot k$ is a perfect square, what is the minimum value of k?

A) 5 B) 7 C) 15 D) 21 E) 35

Solution. Using $n! = n \cdot (n-1)!$, we can easily have the prime factorization of the following numbers:

$$2! = 2, \quad 3! = 2 \cdot 3, \quad 4! = 2^3 \cdot 3, \quad 5! = 2^3 \cdot 3 \cdot 5, \quad 6! = 2^4 \cdot 3^2 \cdot 5,$$

$$7! = 2^4 \cdot 3^2 \cdot 5 \cdot 7, \quad 8! = 2^7 \cdot 3^2 \cdot 5 \cdot 7, \quad 9! = 2^7 \cdot 3^4 \cdot 5 \cdot 7, \quad 10! = 2^8 \cdot 3^4 \cdot 5^2 \cdot 7.$$

Thus,

$$1! \cdot 2! \cdot 3! \cdots 10! = 2^{38} \cdot 3^{17} \cdot 5^7 \cdot 7^4.$$

Hence, the minimum value of k which makes the given product a perfect square is $k = 3 \cdot 5 = 15$. The answer is $\boxed{C}$.

Problem 7. A fair tetrahedral die, whose faces are numbered 1, 2, 3 and 4 is rolled three times. What is the probability that the sum of the numbers rolled is 8?

A) $\dfrac{3}{16}$ B) $\dfrac{3}{32}$ C) $\dfrac{13}{32}$ D) $\dfrac{23}{32}$ E) None of the preceding

Solution. Let (a, b, c) be the outcome when a tetrahedral die is rolled three times. The number of possible outcomes is $4^3 = 64$. However, $a + b + c = 8$ if and only if (a, b, c) is either $(4, 3, 1)$, $(4, 2, 2)$, $(3, 3, 2)$ or their symmetries. Thus, the number of outcomes where $a + b + c = 8$ is $3! + \dfrac{3!}{2!} + \dfrac{3!}{2!} = 12$. So its probability is $\dfrac{12}{64} = \dfrac{3}{16}$. The answer is $\boxed{A}$.

Problem 8. The area of each face of cube A is 8 units^2. The volume of cube B is 75% less than the volume of cube A. What is the volume of cube B in unit^3?

191

Solutions for Practice Exam 10

A) $4\sqrt{2}$

B) $\dfrac{8}{3}$

C) $12\sqrt{2}$

D) $\dfrac{\sqrt{2}}{2}$

E) None of the preceding

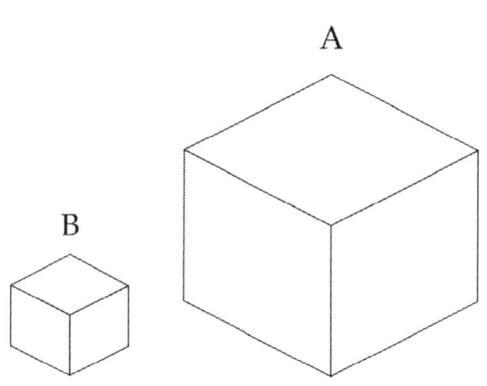

Solution. Let a be the side length of cube A. Since the area of each face of cube A is 8 unit^2, that is, $a^2 = 8$, we have $a = 2\sqrt{2}$. Hence, the volume of cube A is $a^3 = 16\sqrt{2}$. Since the volume of cube B is 75% less than the volume of cube A, that is, $1 - 75\% = \%25 = 1/4$ of the volume of cube A, it is $\dfrac{16\sqrt{2}}{4} = 4\sqrt{2}$ unit^3. The answer is $\boxed{A}$. □

Problem 9. Suppose a and b are non-zero real numbers such that $ax + by = a^2 - ab + b^2$ and $ax - by = a^2 - b^2$. What is the value of $x + y$?

A) $a + \dfrac{b}{4}$ B) $b + \dfrac{a}{4}$ C) $b + \dfrac{a}{2}$ D) $a + \dfrac{b}{3}$ E) $\dfrac{a+b}{2}$

Solution. Notice that

$$ax = \frac{1}{2}\left([a^2 - ab + b^2] + [a^2 - b^2]\right) = a^2 - \frac{ab}{2} \implies x = a - \frac{b}{2}$$

and

$$by = \frac{1}{2}\left([a^2 - ab + b^2] - [a^2 - b^2]\right) = b^2 - \frac{ab}{2} \implies y = b - \frac{a}{2}.$$

Hence, $x + y = \dfrac{a+b}{2}$. The answer is $\boxed{E}$. □

Problem 10. For how many positive integer values of x is the expression $\dfrac{x^2 - 7x + 60}{x}$ an integer?

A) 24 B) 16 C) 12 D) 10 E) 8

Solution. Notice that

$$\frac{x^2 - 7x + 60}{x} = x - 7 + \frac{60}{x}.$$

Therefore, the expression is an integer if and only if 60 is divisible by x. Since the number of positive divisors of $60 = 2^2 \cdot 3 \cdot 5$ is $(2+1) \cdot (1+1) \cdot (1+1) = 12$, there are 12 positive integer values for x. The answer is $\boxed{C}$. □

Solutions for Practice Exam 10

Problem 11. Starting with K, the word KEEP can be formed by moving either horizontally, vertically, or diagonally from square to square in the grid. How many different paths can be followed to form KEEP?

A) 64
B) 72
C) 80
D) 88
E) 96

P	P	P	P	P
P	E	E	E	P
P	E	K	E	P
P	E	E	E	P
P	P	P	P	P

Solution. Denote the E's on the diagonal as E_d, and the others E's as E_s. That is, if we move horizontally or vertically from K, then $K \to E_s$, otherwise, $K \to E_d$. For the second move, we have $E_d \to E_s$ in 2 ways, $E_s \to E_s$ in 2 ways, or $E_s \to E_d$ in 2 ways. For the third move, $E_s \to P$ in 3 ways but $E_d \to P$ in 5 ways. Therefore,

P	P	P	P	P
P	E_d	E_s	E_d	P
P	E_s	K	E_s	P
P	E_d	E_s	E_d	P
P	P	P	P	P

$$K \to E_d \to E_s \to P \quad \text{in } 4 \cdot 2 \cdot 3 = 24 \text{ ways,}$$
$$K \to E_s \to E_s \to P \quad \text{in } 4 \cdot 2 \cdot 3 = 24 \text{ ways,}$$
$$K \to E_s \to E_d \to P \quad \text{in } 4 \cdot 2 \cdot 5 = 40 \text{ ways.}$$

Therefore, the number of ways to form KEEP is 88. The answer is $\boxed{D}$. □

Problem 12. How many of the following five shapes could be the shape of the region where two triangles overlap?

I. equilateral triangle
II. regular pentagon
III. regular hexagon
IV. square
V. kite

A) 1
B) 2
C) 3
D) 4
E) 5

Solution. All of them are possible. We can find an example for each given shape by thinking in the opposite way: for each given shape, can we find two triangles which overlap to from the given shape? It is possible to get an answer when we start drawing the shape and then extend some sides of the shape to get two triangles.

Solutions for Practice Exam 10

For the first shape, take an equilateral triangle △ABC. Extend the sides $\overline{AB}$ and $\overline{AC}$ to some points D and E, respectively. Then △ABC is where △BCE and △ACD overlap.

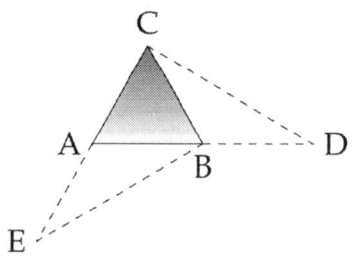

For the second shape, take a regular pentagon ABCDE. Firstly, extend the sides $\overline{CD}$ and $\overline{DE}$, and then intersect them with AB to get points G and F, respectively. Secondly, extend the sides $\overline{AE}$ and $\overline{BC}$, and then intersect them to get the point H. Also pick some points I and J on those lines. Then, ABCDE is where △DFG and △HIJ overlap.

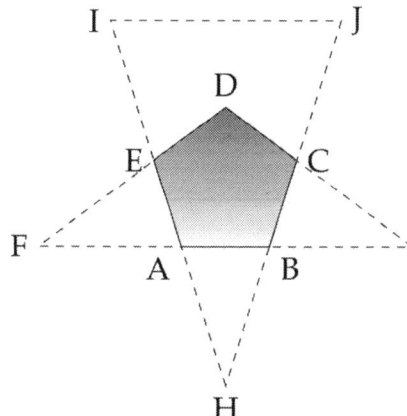

Follow a similar method to obtain the remaining three shapes:

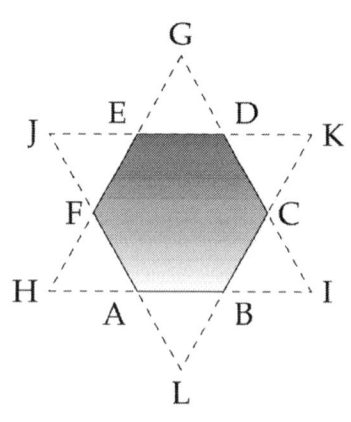
3. Regular Hexagon

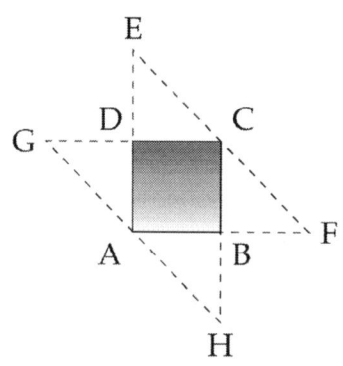
4. Square

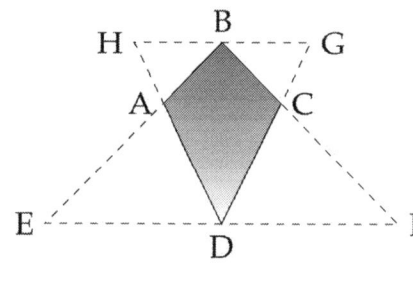
5. Kite

The answer is $\boxed{E}$. □

Problem 13. Let A, B and C be three digits so that the sum of the two-digit numbers AB, BC and CA equals the three-digit number ABC. What is A + B + C?

A) 12 B) 18 C) 19 D) 20 E) 23

Solution. Notice that

$$AB + BC + CA = ABC \implies 11(A + B + C) = ABC.$$

Solutions for Practice Exam 10

So ABC is a multiple of 11. On the other hand, we have

$$ABC = 11(A + B + C) \leq 297.$$

because A, B and C are digits, i.e. $A, B, C \leq 9$. As we check all three digit numbers less than 297 and satisfying $ABC = 11(A+B+C)$, we see that $ABC = 198$ and therefore $A + B + C = 18$. The answer is $\boxed{B}$. □

Problem 14. How many perfect cubes lie between $2^9 + 1$ and $2^{15} + 1$, inclusive?

A) 20 B) 24 C) 26 D) 28 E) 31

Solution. Notice that $8^3 < 2^9 + 1 < 9^3$ and $32^3 = (2^5)^3 < 2^{15} + 1 < (2^5 + 1)^3$. Therefore, the perfect cubes between $2^9 + 1$ and $2^{15} + 1$ are $9^3, 8^3, \ldots, 32^3$. Thus, there are $32 - 9 + 1 = 24$ such perfect cubes. The answer is $\boxed{B}$. □

Problem 15. Suppose a, b, and c are positive integers such that $a + 9b + 15c = 55$. Find the total number of (a, b, c) triples.

A) 3 B) 4 C) 6 D) 7 E) 8

Solution. As $15c < 55$, the value of c is either 3, 2 or 1. Then

$$c = 3 \implies a + 9b = 10 \implies (a, b) = (1, 1).$$
$$c = 2 \implies a + 9b = 25 \implies (a, b) = (7, 2) \text{ or } (16, 1).$$
$$c = 1 \implies a + 9b = 40 \implies (a, b) = (4, 4) \text{ or } (13, 3) \text{ or } (22, 2) \text{ or } (31, 1).$$

Thus, there are 7 triples. The answer is $\boxed{D}$. □

Problem 16. A circle with center O is tangent to $\triangle ABC$ at K, L, and M. If $AM = 8$, $AB = 11$, and $BC = 10$, what is the area of $\triangle ABC$?

A) $12\sqrt{21}$
B) $12\sqrt{3}$
C) $9\sqrt{6}$
D) 24
E) None of the preceding

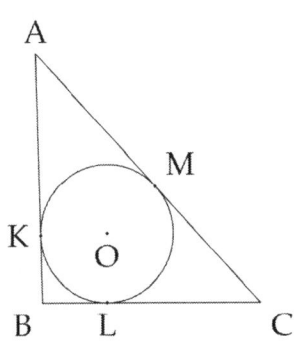

Solutions for Practice Exam 10

Solution. We have
$$AK = AM = 8,$$
$$BK = BL = AB - AK = 11 - 8 = 3,$$
$$CL = CM = BC - BL = 10 - 3 = 7.$$
Thus, $AC = AM + CM = 8 + 7 = 15$. Finally, using the Heron's formula, the area of $\triangle ABC$ is
$$\sqrt{18 \cdot (18-11) \cdot (18-15) \cdot (18-10)} = 12\sqrt{21}.$$
The answer is $\boxed{A}$. □

Problem 17. x and y are two numbers such that $y < |y| < x$. What is the simplified version of $|x+y| - |x| + |y|$?

A) 0 B) $2x + 2y$ C) $2x$ D) $2y$ E) $2x - 2y$

Solution. Since $y < |y| < x$, we have $y < 0 < x$ and so $-y = |y| < x$, i.e. $0 < x + y$. Thus,
$$|x+y| - |x| + |y| = (x+y) - (x) + (-y) = 0.$$
The answer is $\boxed{A}$. □

Problem 18. Let $O(n)$ denote the sum of the odd digits of n. For example, $O(2019) = 1 + 9 = 10$. What is $O(1) + O(2) + O(3) + ... + O(98) + O(99)$?

A) 300 B) 350 C) 400 D) 450 E) 500

Solution. It is clear that $O(1) + O(2) + ... + O(9) = 1 + 3 + 5 + 7 + 9 = 25$. For two-digit numbers, we have $O(ab) = O(a) + O(b)$, that is, $O(ab) = O(a) + O(b)$ when a is odd, and $O(ab) = O(b)$ when a is even. Notice that we always have $O(b)$ whatever a is. Besides, there are 10 two-digit numbers for each $a = 1, 3, 5, 7, 9$. Thus,
$$O(1) + O(2) + ... + O(99) = \left(\sum_{a=0}^{9} \sum_{b=0}^{9} O(b)\right) + \left(10 \cdot \sum_{a \text{ is odd}} O(a)\right)$$
$$= \sum_{a=0}^{9} 25 + 10 \cdot 25$$
$$= 250 + 250 = 500$$
The answer is $\boxed{E}$. □

Problem 19. Three standard six-sided dice are rolled, and the sum S is calculated. What is the probability that $S(21 - S) < 80$?

A) $\frac{1}{27}$ B) $\frac{5}{81}$ C) $\frac{13}{216}$ D) $\frac{1}{9}$ E) None of the preceding

Solutions for Practice Exam 10

Solution. We have

$$S(21 - S) < 80 \implies 0 < S^2 - 21S + 80 = (S - 5)(S - 16).$$

The inequality is satisfied when $S - 5$ and $S - 16$ are both positive or negative at the same time. That is, $S > 16$ or $S < 5$. The probability that $S > 16$ is

$$\frac{1+3}{6^3} = \frac{4}{216} = \frac{1}{54}$$

by considering $(6,6,6)$ and $(6,6,5)$ and their symmetries. On the other hand, the probability that $S < 5$ is

$$\frac{3+1}{6^3} = \frac{4}{216} = \frac{1}{54}$$

by considering $(2,1,1)$ and $(1,1,1)$ and their symmetries. Thus, the probability that $S > 16$ or $S < 5$ is $\frac{1}{54} + \frac{1}{54} = \frac{1}{27}$. The answer is $\boxed{A}$. □

Problem 20. ABC is a triangle with $AB = AD = BE$. $m\angle A = 114°$ and $m\angle B = 60°$. Find $m\angle EDC$.

A) 112°

B) 117°

C) 122°

D) 127°

E) 150°

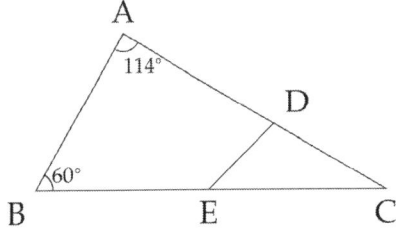

Solution. As $AB = BE$ and $m\angle B = 60$, we have that $\triangle ABE$ is equilateral. As $AB = AD = BE$, we have $AE = AD$. Also

$$m\angle EAD = m\angle BAD - m\angle BAE = 114° - 60° = 54°.$$

Since $\triangle AED$ is an isosceles triangle with $m\angle EAD = 54°$, we have

$$m\angle AED = m\angle ADE = \frac{180° - 54°}{2} = 63°.$$

Finally, $m\angle EDC = 180° - m\angle ADE = 180° - 63° = 117°$. The answer is $\boxed{B}$. □

Problem 21. How many real number solutions does the equation $5^x x^2 + 125 = 5^{x+2} + 5x^2$ have?

A) 0   B) 1   C) 3   D) 5   E) Infinitely Many

197

Solutions for Practice Exam 10

Solution.

$$5^x x^2 + 125 = 5^{x+2} + 5x^2 \implies 5^x(x^2 - 25) - 5(x^2 - 25) = 0 \implies (5^x - 5)(x^2 - 25) = 0.$$

Thus, either $5^x = 5$ or $x^2 - 25 = 0$. In other words, x is either 1, 5 or −5. There are three solutions. The answer is $\boxed{C}$. □

Problem 22. Numbers of the form 2020a + b such that a and b are integers with $1 \leq a < b \leq 2019$ and $b^2 - a^2$ is divisible by 673 are written in increasing order as thus:

$$1 \cdot 2020 + 672 = 2692, \quad 1 \cdot 2020 + 674 = 2694, \quad 1 \cdot 2020 + 1345 = 3365, \quad 1 \cdot 2020 + 1347 = 3367, \ldots$$

What is the 2020-th number in the sequence?

A) $405 \cdot 2019$ B) $422 \cdot 2019$ C) $506 \cdot 2019$ D) $1011 \cdot 2019$ E) None of the preceding

Solution. Since 673 is prime, either b − a or b + a is divisible by 673. For $a = 1, 2, \ldots, 336$, there are 5 such numbers, and for $a \geq 337$ there are 4 such numbers. As $2020 = 5 \cdot 336 + 4 \cdot 85$, we have $a = 336 + 85 = 421$ and therefore the 2020-th number is $421 \cdot 2020 + 2019 - 421 = 421(2020 - 1) + 2019 = 422 \cdot 2019$. The answer is $\boxed{B}$. □

Problem 23. All positive integers whose digits are all even are written in increasing order in the base ten system. 2, 4, 6, 8, 20, 22, 24, 26, 28, 40, 42, 44, 46, 48, 60, ... Find the 499th number of this pattern.

A) 4444   B) 4666   C) 4888   D) 6666   E) 6888

Solution. The even digits are 0, 2, 4, 6 and 8. For a three-digit number abc (by also allowing 0s for a, b, c), there are $5 \cdot 5 \cdot 5 = 125$ such numbers. Then there are

$$\underbrace{124}_{\#\text{"0abc"}} + \underbrace{125}_{\#\text{"2abc"}} + \underbrace{125}_{\#\text{"4abc"}} + \underbrace{125}_{\#\text{"6abc"}} = 499$$

such numbers up to 8000. Therefore, the 499-th number is 6888, which comes just before 8000. The answer is $\boxed{E}$. □

Problem 24. In a semicircle with center O, $m\angle OAC = 52°$ and $AC = CD = CE$. What is $m\angle DCE$?

A) 24°
B) 28°
C) 32°
D) 36°
E) 40°

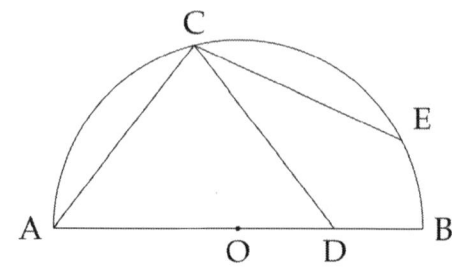

198

Solutions for Practice Exam 10

Solution. As m∠OAC = 52°, the arc angle of BC is $2 \cdot 52° = 104°$. Then, the arc angle of AC is $180° - 104° = 76°$. So m∠CEA = $\frac{76°}{2} = 38°$. As △ACD and △ACE are isosceles triangles, we have

$$m\angle ACD = 180° - 2 \cdot 52° = 76° \quad \text{and} \quad m\angle ACE = 180° - 2 \cdot 38° = 104°.$$

Therefore, m∠DCE = m∠ACE − m∠ACD = 104° − 76° = 28°. The answer is $\boxed{B}$. □

Problem 25. Suppose x and y are real numbers that satisfy $2x^2 - 3y = -\frac{17}{2}$ and $y^2 - 4x = 7$. What is the value of $x + y$?

A) $\frac{7}{2}$ B) $\frac{5}{4}$ C) $\frac{3}{2}$ D) $\frac{1}{4}$ E) None of the preceding

Solution. As $4x^2 - 6y = -17$ and $y^2 - 4x = 7$, we have

$$0 = (4x^2 - 6y) + (y^2 - 4x) + 10 = (4x^2 - 4x + 1) + (y^2 - 6y + 9) = (2x - 1)^2 + (y - 3)^2.$$

Then $2x - 1 = 0$ and $y - 3 = 0$. In other words, $x = \frac{1}{2}$ and $y = 3$. Thus, $x + y = \frac{7}{2}$. The answer is $\boxed{A}$.

Alternative Solution. As $y^2 - 4x = 7$, we have

$$y^2 - 4x = 7 \implies 4x = y^2 - 7 \implies 16x^2 = (y^2 - 7)^2.$$

On the other hand, as $4x^2 - 6y = -17$, we have

$$4x^2 - 6y = -17 \implies 16x^2 - 24y = -68 \implies 16x^2 = 24y - 68.$$

Therefore $(y^2 - 7)^2 = 24y - 68$, i.e. $y^4 - 14y^2 - 24y + 117 = 0$. The solution for the last equation is $y = 3$, hence $x = \frac{1}{2}$. Thus, $x + y = \frac{7}{2}$, and the answer is $\boxed{A}$. □

Practice Test 1				
1-C	6-B	11-A	16-B	21-B
2-C	7-D	12-A	17-D	22-D
3-A	8-D	13-B	18-C	23-D
4-B	9-D	14-D	19-A	24-C
5-C	10-C	15-B	20-C	25-C

Practice Test 2				
1-D	6-D	11-D	16-C	21-C
2-B	7-D	12-D	17-A	22-C
3-D	8-D	13-C	18-A	23-D
4-A	9-A	14-E	19-E	24-A
5-B	10-E	15-A	20-A	25-A

Practice Test 3				
1-C	6-B	11-B	16-D	21-A
2-A	7-B	12-B	17-A	22-B
3-C	8-B	13-D	18-D	23-A
4-B	9-C	14-D	19-E	24-A
5-A	10-C	15-D	20-D	25-B

Practice Test 4				
1-C	6-E	11-C	16-A	21-B
2-B	7-D	12-B	17-D	22-E
3-A	8-A	13-A	18-E	23-C
4-B	9-B	14-A	19-E	24-C
5-D	10-D	15-D	20-E	25-B

Practice Test 5				
1-	6-B	11-C	16-A	21-B
2-	7-E	12-A	17-B	22-A
3-	8-E	13-D	18-C	23-D
4-	9-A	14-B	19-B	24-D
5-	10-B	15-B	20-D	25-B

Practice Test 6				
1-A	6-E	11-B	16-A	21-C
2-E	7-A	12-E	17-A	22-B
3-C	8-D	13-A	18-C	23-E
4-B	9-D	14-B	19-C	24-B
5-B	10-D	15-D	20-B	25-D

Practice Test 7				
1-A	6-B	11-D	16-A	21-B
2-E	7-C	12-B	17-A	22-C
3-D	8-B	13-C	18-C	23-B
4-C	9-E	14-E	19-C	24-D
5-B	10-D	15-A	20-E	25-D

Practice Test 8				
1-D	6-A	11-B	16-B	21-C
2-D	7-E	12-E	17-D	22-A
3-D	8-D	13-C	18-C	23-A
4-E	9-B	14-B	19-E	24-C
5-D	10-E	15-A	20-C	25-B

Practice Test 9				
1-B	6-D	11-E	16-D	21-A
2-A	7-C	12-D	17-D	22-A
3-B	8-E	13-A	18-C	23-E
4-C	9-B	14-A	19-E	24-B
5-A	10-C	15-E	20-B	25-C

Practice Test 10				
1-C	6-C	11-D	16-A	21-C
2-C	7-A	12-E	17-A	22-B
3-E	8-A	13-B	18-E	23-E
4-E	9-E	14-B	19-A	24-B
5-C	10-C	15-D	20-B	25-A

Made in the USA
Las Vegas, NV
07 September 2021